D0114441

Soldiers
of the Old Army

TEXAS A&M UNIVERSITY
MILITARY HISTORY SERIES
15

Soldiers
of the Old Army

BY VICTOR VOGEL

Texas A&M University Press

COLLEGE STATION

For the regulars

WHO LOVED THE OLD ARMY

AND CALLED IT HOME

The paper used in this book meets the minimum requirements of the
American National Standard for Permanence of Paper for Printed Library
Materials, Z39.48-1984. Binding materials have been chosen for durability.

LIBRARY OF CONGRESS CATALOGING-IN-PUBLICATION DATA

Vogel, Victor, 1909–
    Soldiers of the old army / by Victor Vogel. — 1st ed.
      p. cm. — (Texas A&M University military history
      series; no. 15)
    ISBN 0-89096-420-3 (alk. paper)
    1. United States. Army—Military life—History—20th
      century.
    I. Title. II. Series: Texas A&M University military
      history series; 15.
    U766.V64 1990
    355.1 ' 0973 ' 09043—dc20   89–20314
                                     CIP

Contents

Illustrations

Introduction

Throughout the history of the United States it has been the policy of the government to demobilize the army as quickly as possible after a war and send the soldiers home. Following World War I the country reverted to isolationism and the army was quickly reduced to the minimum size required to carry out limited overseas obligations and to provide a skeleton force for the defense of the United States at home. The basis for the organization of our army between the two world wars was the National Defense Act of 1920.

The purpose of the act was to establish an army structure based on the traditional principle that the citizen soldier would be able to defend our nation under any of the possible conditions which were foreseen. At the time, the scope of operations of World War II and its demands on the work force could not be imagined.

The maximum authorized strength of the regular army was set at 17,717 officers and 280,000 enlisted men, but it was never that large until 1940, when the Selective Service and Training Act became law. Universal military service was rejected, and all services were required to depend solely on volunteers. The act was not fully funded by Congress, and until 1939 the actual strength of the regular army never exceeded 12,000 officers and 118,750 enlisted men. The Philippine Scouts, a force of 6,400, also a part of the U.S. forces, was restricted to service in the Philippine Islands.

Included in the total number authorized were men of the Army Air Service, which became the Army Air Corps in 1925, and of the Coast Artillery Corps, which manned fixed defenses at strategic locations. In addition, the regular service furnished advisers to National Guard and Reserve Officer Training Corps (ROTC) units. When the Civilian Conservation Corps camps were authorized in 1933, the army assigned officers and enlisted men to administrative and supply duties in these camps. This duty reduced the number of men available for infantry, artillery, and cavalry field units, which remained below strength.

The dismantling of the army after World War I, the failure to fund the forces authorized by the National Defense Act of 1920, and the inclusion of branches of the service not available to the ground forces left the army stripped to the bare bones as a fighting force. Throughout the 1920s and 1930s these policies determined the organization and training of the regular army.

The major active units of the ground forces authorized under the 1920 act were the 1st, 2d, and 3d Infantry Divisions and the 1st Cavalry Division (horse). In addition, a number of separate regiments and independent battalions were stationed at small posts in the United States and in territories overseas. Regiments were often broken up into garrisons consisting of a few companies. For example, Fort Crook, Nebraska, was manned by two rifle companies of the 17th Infantry. Other companies of the 17th were located at Fort Leavenworth, Kansas. The 15th Infantry was in China, the 22d in the Philippines, the 65th in Puerto Rico, the 6th at Jefferson Barracks, Missouri, and the 24th (a regiment of black troops) at Fort Huachuca, Arizona.

The largest concentration of troops of the regular army was in Texas, where the 2d Infantry Division was stationed at Fort Sam Houston near San Antonio, and regiments of the 1st Cavalry Division were scattered along the border with Mexico at the frontier forts of Brown, MacIntosh, Ringgold, and Bliss.

Of these, only Fort Sam Houston at San Antonio and Fort Bliss at El Paso are now active posts.

The 1st Infantry Division was billeted in New York State, and the 3d was in Washington State.

The 2d Division was not intact because the 4th Brigade was located at Fort Francis E. Warren, Wyoming, with a regiment of artillery. Still, in the 1930s, the combined strength of the 3d Infantry Brigade, two regiments of the artillery brigade, plus the division headquarters and special troops, gave the 2d Division the largest number of troops at one post.

Weapons, uniforms, and equipment were the same as those used in World War I. The cavalry rode horses. The artillery pulled guns with six-horse teams. The infantry marched fifteen miles a day and used mules to pull supply wagons. There was no increase in pay between 1922 and 1942. It was only when war began in Europe in 1939 that changes were made to modernize our forces, and these came gradually.

This was the United States Army when I enlisted in the 9th Infantry Regiment in April, 1934, at Fort Sam Houston, Texas. Growing up in southeastern Missouri was good basic training for a boy interested in a military career. It was an ideal place for an outdoor life, with forests to roam, caves to explore, and rivers to swim, fish, and canoe. Learning to use a rifle was part of one's education, and camping was a favorite form of recreation. With that background army life presented no hardship.

Why anyone would choose a vocation in which the pay was low, the outlook for advancement uncertain, and the business neglected by its owners is explained in the following pages.

Soldiers
of the Old Army

CHAPTER ONE

The Regulars

It was a school, an athletic club, an orphans' home, and a boys' camp all rolled together, which wasn't bad, considering that a man got room and board, his clothes, and twenty-one dollars a month. Officially it was known as the United States Army. The time was the 1930s.

Twenty-one dollars was pay for a private, but there was opportunity for advancement if a man stayed on long enough, for he might make private first class on his first enlistment and maybe become a corporal in eight or ten years. It was no place for an in-and-outer. A popular barracks story illustrates the point.

The men of an infantry company gathered about the bulletin board to read the order promoting a private to private first class. "What is this man's army coming to?" one soldier complained in disgust. "Hogan is promoted to first class and he only has six years' service. I'm going to transfer to a good outfit."

It was not entirely a joke, for a survey of the 2d Infantry Division at Fort Sam Houston, Texas, in the mid-1930s showed the average length of service for privates to be three years; that of privates first class, five years; corporals, twelve years; and sergeants, eighteen years. Sergeants of the first three grades, the elite of the noncommissioned officers corps, averaged twenty-four years of service. It took determination to rise in the ranks of the regulars, and promotions, once attained, were not lightly treated.

It is true that there were exceptions, as in the case of a soldier known as "Swede" in Headquarters Company, 3d Infantry Brigade, a mule skinner with several enlistments behind him. The army used horses and mules in those days, and a mule skinner held an exalted position in the infantry because he could ride instead of walk. He also had the rank of private first class, which paid thirty dollars a month, with an added specialist sixth class rating that went with the job and was worth another three dollars a month. This put a mule skinner in the upper financial bracket, and it gave a man a lot of prestige as well. A foot soldier looked up to the driver sitting on the box seat of a supply wagon. There were certain other advantages such as being able to hide a bottle of bourbon in the oat bin where the Old Man never looked when he inspected stables.

Swede, as a qualified mule skinner and with sufficient service, was entitled to the rank and was duly advanced to private first class in company orders. With his first increase in pay, however, success went to this head and he celebrated in a manner that was not in the best interest of the service or himself. He got drunk in a local saloon, picked a fight with another soldier, and got whipped. Unfortunately for both parties to the fray, the military police arrived on the scene and hauled them back to Fort Sam. Next morning the company commander called Swede to the orderly room, demanded an explanation, and, after listening to the essential facts, announced, "Private first class, you are hereby reduced to private," and Swede was back at the bottom again.

Whether the reduction was for drunkenness, fighting, or getting whipped was never revealed and Swede didn't know either. The following month he was promoted to private first class once more, but before long he was busted back to private again. Swede was a good soldier, knew his job, and loved the army, but he couldn't stand success. He just wasn't cut out to shoulder so much responsibility.

In 1934 the United States Army consisted of 12,000 officers and 118,750 enlisted men, more or less, including the aviation service, which was called the Army Air Corps. There was also a force of 6,400 Philippine Scouts, organized for duty in the Philippine Islands only.

Douglas MacArthur was chief of staff of the army at the time, and he held that job until 1935, when his four-year tour was up. Then, the story goes, he could have stayed on active duty as a major general, but he wouldn't take a reduction in rank from full general and for that reason he retired from the United States Army. Strange as it may seem, he then became field marshal of the Philippine Army, the only U.S. officer to hold such a rank. One of his staff officers was a major named Dwight D. Eisenhower.

A lot of paper with MacArthur's name on it came down through channels—general orders, special orders, bulletins—"By order of the Secretary of War, Douglas MacArthur, Chief of Staff." To me, a private, it was a name on a piece of paper, but I read some of those papers out of curiosity and they seemed important.

To most regulars, it wasn't important who the chief of staff was, or the company commander, for that matter. Officers came and went, but the company, the "outfit," as it was called, kept on because of or in spite of them. The veteran regular who made the army his home took it one day at a time and didn't worry about tomorrow. When his enlistment expired, he reenlisted the next day and continued the march. Each had his own reasons. Some enlisted because they needed a job and it was the only thing they could find that suited them, others because it was an escape from responsibility into a well-ordered world where everything was provided for them; still others, and there were many of them, chose the army as a career in which they expected to be of service to their country. All had one thing in common—they were volunteers.

When a recruit joined the army he enlisted for the regiment

of his choice and went immediately to that regiment. He received basic training as a member of the company, troop, or battery to which he was permanently assigned. Until he completed this training under the supervision of a noncommissioned officer, usually a corporal, the new soldier performed no other duty.

There was no set time for training a recruit, and a man progressed as quickly as he could learn the basic details of soldiering. For some this was only a matter of two or three weeks; for others it took months. When the recruit was turned to duty he was assigned to a squad, placed on the duty roster and the guard roster, and took his turn at all duties performed by members of the unit. Each soldier received advanced training as the unit took part in field exercises, fired on the range, or took special training required by the schedule, which was planned a year at a time.

Specialists, such as communications personnel, headquarters clerks, bakers, cooks, and buglers, were selected from line companies and given special training for those jobs as vacancies occurred. Vacancies in regimental bands were filled by recruiting qualified musicians especially for those jobs.

A man enlisted for three years, and this meant three years' "good time." Any time lost that was not in line of duty was tacked on to the end of the term of enlistment. If a man was absent without leave, he had to make good the number of days he was gone plus the time he spent in the guardhouse as punishment. Bad time in the hospital as the result of venereal disease had to be made up, as was time in the hospital as a result of an accident not in line of duty. If a soldier was hurt in a brawl and went to the hospital for repairs, it was not in line of duty and he had to make it good. There was no pay for such bad time, but all was not lost because a soldier was entitled to three square meals and a bunk wherever he was.

It was not uncommon for soldiers to serve three and a half to four years, or more, on an enlistment to make up bad time, but most hit it on the button and received an honorable discharge at the end of their normal term of service.

The reenlistment rate was high, although there were no bonuses, no promises of promotion, and no additional incentives. A man could reenlist to fill his own vacancy, with the rank he held at the time of discharge, or he could go to another outfit and sign up as a private. He didn't take his rank with him if he had one, and usually a soldier had to be dissatisfied to change outfits.

There was one exception to the three-year term of service—a one-year enlistment to take the examinations for entry to the United States Military Academy at West Point, New York. A high school graduate who met the physical requirements could sign up to attend a preparatory training course leading to an appointment to the academy if he completed the course with a satisfactory grade. It was a tough grind, and few men got to West Point by that route, but the opportunity was there and some made it. A man who failed to complete the preparatory course was required to finish his twelve-month enlistment in a regular unit.

A unique feature of the pre–World War II army was the purchased discharge, a right that passed into military history with the horse. After twelve months' good time, a soldier could buy his discharge for the cash price of $120, no questions asked. After two years the price went down to $100, then it dropped in increments of $10 a year to a minimum of $30. After purchasing a discharge, which was honorable, a soldier who reenlisted started over in the same price scale and there was no legal limit to the number of times an enlisted man could buy out. More than one soldier had his getaway money salted down in a safe place against the day when, for one reason or another, he wanted to buy out and face the cold, cruel civilian world.

Dishonorable discharges were the result of conviction by a general court-martial for a serious offense such as murder, robbery, larceny, or desertion. The most common of these was desertion, but the culprits were seldom apprehended and the army made no attempt to find them. If a man was absent without leave for more than ninety days he was dropped from the rolls and forgotten.

When the draft began in 1940, the roundup netted a number of those old deserters, but all were forgiven when they signed up for the duration of the war plus six months. One of these draftees who had deserted in 1938 was called up in 1942 and assigned to my outfit. He promptly made a claim for back pay, which he said was owed him when he "went over the hill" (a phrase that meant a soldier had gone AWOL or deserted). To his disappointment the claim was disapproved.

Most units went for years without any of the men committing a serious infraction of regulations, and courts-martial were rare. In a five-year stretch one man was dishonorably discharged from Headquarters Company, 3d Infantry Brigade. He was convicted for having stolen from a buddy a book of ten moving picture theater tickets worth $1.20. It was a harsh verdict, but regulars did not want to serve with a man who would steal from a comrade.

Minor violations were handled within the company by "company punishment," which meant restriction to the post or barracks or extra duty on Sundays or holidays. Being late for formation, wearing improper uniform, or having a dirty rifle fell in this category. In repeated or more severe cases the penalty was reduction in rank or loss of specialist's rating. Either of these was considered a fate worse than death, for it hit the soldier where it hurt the most—in the wallet. But a specialist's rating could be recovered more easily.

For the most part, the regular army enlisted man of pre–World War II days was reliable, cheerful, willing, respectful, physically tough, proud of his outfit, and above all, patriotic. If there were horseplay and mischief at times, it was because he was young and led an active life. He considered his profession an honorable one and service to his country serious business.

Maybe the reason for this positive attitude was the time. The

Depression of the 1930s had hit the country hard, but most Americans were proud and hesitated to take charity or go on welfare. Patriotism was a virtue, and disrespect to the flag was not tolerated. The lifestyle of the military services did not appeal to many young men, but there was never a shortage of volunteers to fill the ranks of the regulars.

Many a soldier was heard to say, "every day in the army is like Sunday on the farm."

CHAPTER TWO

Garrison Duty

At six in the morning, every day except Sundays and holidays, or when we were in the field, the 9th Infantry drum and bugle corps woke the regiment with a tune we irreverently called "My Old Man." Maybe that wasn't its title, maybe it didn't have one, but that is what we called it, and we made up words to go with the music.

"My old man was an infantryman, what in hell was your old man?" the second platoon of Company A would bellow off-key as we rolled out of the blankets for reveille. The other platoons of the outfit would groan and mutter obscenities, but it was a good way to start the day.

The drum and bugle boys would march around the quadrangle formed by our barracks until all fourteen companies of the regiment fell in, answered roll call, and were reported by the noncommissioned officer in charge to the officer of the day, who stood out in the middle of the square where he could see what was going on. This was a ritual that never varied, and a soldier soon became so accustomed to it that he could make reveille formation drunk, sober, or half asleep.

The barracks of the 9th Infantry at Fort Sam Houston were comfortable, three-story, stucco buildings, which had been built in 1929. The ground floor housed the company offices, the kitchen and dining room, and the recreation room, called the dayroom. Sleeping quarters and washrooms were on the second and third floors; privates used the large squad rooms, and there were individual rooms for single noncommissioned officers. The basement was used for storage of supplies and included a small-caliber firing range for indoor target practice.

In contrast to these modern buildings, the barracks of the 23d Infantry, also stationed at Fort Sam Houston, were built between 1885 and 1891. Their mess halls and kitchens were separated from the living quarters, which was especially inconvenient in bad weather. The latrines were also a distance away, which on cold and rainy nights worked a real hardship on men with weak kidneys who had filled up on beer before turning in.

The quadrangle is the oldest building on the post and is today still much the same as it was in 1876, the year it was completed. The interior has been modernized and the old observation ports, or small windows, described in some records as "loopholes," are still there. The same stone wall encloses the compound, and the clock tower remains in the center of the square. The quadrangle was built as a supply depot and headquarters for the infantry and cavalry troops that patrolled the Southwest following the Civil War, and it has housed the headquarters of corps areas and field armies since 1921, when the depot was moved across the street.

Garrison duty for the infantry in the 1930s followed a routine training schedule that covered close-order drill, extended order or tactical formations, marksmanship, and physical conditioning. Sometimes there would be classroom work or lectures, but these were held to a minimum.

The basic formation was the squad, and all drill, marching, and tactics were centered on the movement of this unit. Theoretically, there were eight men in a squad, although squads were seldom at full strength because men were absent on furlough, in the hospital, or on special duty. The squad leader was a corporal, or an acting corporal in many cases, usually a man with several enlistments on his record.

When I enlisted in Company A, 9th Infantry, in 1934, my squad leader was Cpl. Abner Bickham, an outstanding noncommissioned officer. Abner was a fine-looking soldier, a member of the regimental rifle team, and a superior leader. He knew his job well, had an easy, confident manner, got along with his men, and possessed a keen sense of humor. Members of his squad respected him and felt they were fortunate to have him as their leader.

Each man was required to memorize the movements of all positions in the squad, both close order and extended or tactical order. From time to time each man was given a chance to command the squad to prepare him for promotion when he became qualified and there was a vacancy.

Close-order drill was a precise and serious business. Its purpose was to teach alertness as well as military discipline, and it got people to the right place at the right time. It also required a great deal of instruction, patience, and hours of practice, which is why it was abandoned later in favor of a simpler method of forming the squad in a single line instead of having two ranks of four men each.

The old squad drill was a real challenge, although there were times when it didn't work out as intended. One of the more complicated movements was called "right front into line," in which the company would be marching in a column and at the command all squads would execute a right turn and form a new line at right angles to the original line of march. It wasn't the easiest thing in the book. One morning at drill the acting corporal in charge became rattled on his first try at this maneuver and was befuddled as the squads failed to make the proper turns. "Get where you belong," he shouted as the company commander, a captain, went into shock at this unprofessional behavior and the men executed the movement with military precision.

A routine morning would be spent in close-order drill, tactical drill, use of weapons, and physical training. Special units such as communications platoons, mounted sections, and supply and headquarters clerks worked on those jobs. Sometimes there would be classes on gas warfare, map reading, mob control, message writing, and the like.

One subject of complete disinterest to most soldiers was the "Articles of War," although all were governed by them. Every six months all soldiers were required to attend a class on this subject, conducted by an officer who would read and explain the law governing military personnel. This was punishment in itself, and there was no escape.

On a warm day the monotonous droning of such phrases as "to forfeit all pay and allowances due or to become due," or "shall suffer such other punishment as a court-martial may direct," would put some of the group to sleep. When this happened, the officer-instructor would call the culprit to attention, and he would stand until the class was dismissed, often quickly returning to a sound sleep on his feet.

But there were always a few who listened faithfully to the legal details and studied the book containing the articles, a copy of which was on hand in each company, troop, or battery, available to anyone interested. From time to time these students of military law were called upon, or more often, volunteered, to give advice to their friends who got caught in violation of one of the many rules. These amateur experts were known as guardhouse lawyers, and every outfit had at least one. Sometimes there more than one, and their differences of opinion on the law might be decided by fisticuffs back of the barracks instead of by verbal argument.

Next to women, the subject most frequently discussed was the article that penalized a soldier for being drunk. This always brought up the question, moot and never-ending, as to how to be sure a man was drunk, for there was always the possibility that a soldier might be called as a witness before a court-martial to state whether another soldier was drunk or sober. There were vast differences of opinion on this matter. One argument held that it was impossible to tell if a man was drunk, therefore the article was unconstitutional and a soldier could not legally be tried for this offense, or even accused. For practical reasons not much attention was given to this argument. Too many men did bad time on the charge. Another line of reasoning was much simpler—ask a man's buddies. His closest friends could tell when he was sober, and they could tell when he was drunk because they knew his capacity from experience and when he exceeded that capacity. The flaw in this theory was obvious—no real friend would give testimony that would send a comrade to the guardhouse.

Pvt. Bill Shafer, Headquarters Company, 3d Infantry Brigade, with three enlistments and plenty of experience to qualify him as an expert on sobriety, had an opinion that made sense. "A man is drunk," said Bill, "when he is lying in the grass and can't hang on when the military police try to drag him away."

In addition to training routine, each man would pull a tour of guard duty several times each month. The guard would be divided into three reliefs, each of which was on two hours and off four, alternately walking post and sleeping in the guardhouse.

Guard mount, the formation to change the guard from day to day, could be formal or informal. At the formal ceremony, which took place once a week, there was an inspection of the new guard by the officer of the day, a march-past of the old guard by the new, rousing music played by the regimental band, and a great deal of fanfare. At the informal mount the old and new guards simply fell in, the new guard was inspected, and the old was relieved—no music, no pomp. These formations served a good purpose in putting some color into the otherwise monotonous routine of guard duty.

Sentry posts at Fort Sam Houston were typical of those at other stations, consisting of such strategic places as horse corrals, boxcar sidings, and stacks of hay. My favorite was the haystack. At night, after the officer of the day had made his inspection of the post, I would lean back in the hay, breathing in the sweet aroma of timothy and clover. There are no smells more fragrant than that of high-quality, well-cured hay, and the army bought the best.

Another job that fell to privates with regularity was kitchen police, which, like sentry duty, came around about two or three times a month. Unlike walking post it did not require round-the-clock performance, only a twelve-hour shift.

Normally three men, privates or privates first class, would be assigned to this work from the company duty roster. Two men would assist the cook by making coffee, peeling potatoes, and performing tasks that did not involve the actual preparation of meals. They also did such distasteful jobs as washing pots, scrubbing floors, and cleaning garbage cans. The third man was the dining room orderly, who set the tables and cleaned the dining area when the meal was finished. All three men served table during the meal, seeing that empty service bowls were refilled and pitchers were kept full of coffee, water, tea, or whatever drink was served.

Some soldiers disliked the job, but it wasn't hard work and in bad weather it beat drilling or guard duty. Also there was plenty of coffee at all times and leftover pie was a fringe benefit. No one liked to pull kitchen police on Sundays or holidays, but a man could always find a buddy to take his place for five dollars, the going rate, if there was something important going on that he didn't want to miss, such as a poker game. Since five dollars equaled 25 percent of a private's monthly pay, it indicates the value placed on a day in the kitchen.

A company, troop, or battery would have two cooks, a first and a second, both privates first class with specialists' ratings, and they seldom performed any other duty except to fire their weapons when the unit was on the firing range. The mess sergeant, a three-striper, was in charge of the entire mess.

The mess sergeant of Company A, 9th Infantry, Sergeant Grabowsky, was a marvel at turning out good meals, and the food was equal to that served in the best restaurants in San Antonio. This was partly because of the practice of allowing the mess sergeant to buy food on the open market with the ration allowance for men in the mess. In this way fresh meat and produce could be bought in town and meals varied from the standard quartermaster menu. If a mess sergeant was a good manager, he could save enough money to put on a special feed for the outfit from time to time.

Garrison duty was not all routine, however, and there were frequent parades, guards of honor, full field inspections, and reviews to give variety to the training schedule.

One of the more spectacular ceremonies was the division review. All troops of the 2d Infantry Division, foot, artillery, and service, would form up on the main parade, which was about a mile and a half long and quarter mile wide, with colors flying and brass polished. The bands would play, and the division commander, Major General Bowles, would make a brief inspection of troops before taking his place in the reviewing stand for the march-past. The infantry would lead off on foot, followed by the horse-drawn artillery and the special troops. Then the fun started.

After the foot troops cleared the line of march, the artillery batteries would pass the reviewing stand at a walk. Then, after the first pass, they would swing around and come by again at a trot, raising a cloud of dust that reduced visibility to zero and causing some uncertainty as to where everybody was going. When the horses went past the reviewing stand the second time they knew the show was over, for they learned the routine as well as the men, and it was not unusual for at least one team to head for the stables at a gallop. When this happened others would join them and there would be a race the length of the parade ground. As they passed the infantry barracks, we would cheer them on as the gunners struggled to get their horses under control.

Weekday afternoons were devoted to cleaning up grounds or equipment or other housekeeping chores. Team sports were popular, and, there was usually an athletic contest in the afternoons. If a man did not have any other duty he could be found on the athletic field.

At ten in the evening when the 9th Infantry was in garrison,

16

the bugler of the guard stepped out into the quadrangle and blew tattoo. This signal notified the noncommissioned officer in charge of quarters for each company that it was time to turn out the lights in squad rooms and the dayroom and for everyone in the outfit to quiet down. At a quarter past ten the bugler blew taps, which meant that everything was finished for the day. On a summer night the music would float across the quadrangle and through the open barracks windows with a comforting sound that made a man feel that joining the army was a good choice.

During the night the officer of the day made his rounds to see that order was maintained and sentries were on post. Number One of the guard relief on duty walked in front of the guardhouse. All sentry posts were numbered so that the location could be identified, and Number One was the choice assignment because that sentry didn't have far to walk when the guard was changed. The man selected for Number One had to be alert at all times for a surprise visit by the regimental commander, who might try to catch the guard napping. When this happened, Number One would shout, "Turn out the guard, the Commanding Officer," and the reliefs off duty would dash out of the guardhouse and fall in for the Old Man, who would then make a perfunctory inspection.

Ordinarily, however, Number One's principal duty was to announce the arrival of the new guard when it came on duty in the afternoon. This was done by shouting, "Turn out the guard, armed party." This was only a formality because everyone was waiting impatiently to go off duty and knew that the "armed party" was the new guard. The practice stemmed from the days when a frontier post might be attacked by Indians or Mexicans, and it was kept in the manual as a matter of tradition.

The reliefs off duty slept in the guardroom, to be awakened by the sergeant of the guard when they were to go on sentry duty.

Everyone who was broke or restricted to quarters for some

unrepented military sin hit the sack when the bugler blew taps. The others, those with a few bucks left from payday, who had been to town or to "red-light" Rattlesnake Hill, straggled in throughout the night and got a few hours' bunk time before reveille. The shack men, who had permission to sleep off the post because they were married (or said they were), made it back in time to fall in with the company.

There was no bed check. If a soldier couldn't stand on his feet the next morning, he went on the list of those restricted to quarters and, like the others, did not repent.

First call for reveille the next work day at six o'clock started the cycle once more.

In general, garrison duty prepared soldiers for advanced training in the field. Although some duties did not fit the strict meaning of this requirement. The training program was well designed to keep regular army units in a state of readiness to provide the first line of defense for our country and to train leaders for wartime service.

CHAPTER THREE

In the Field

When Company A, 9th Infantry, moved into the field each man carried his weapons, a full pack, and a cheese sandwich. Those packs were the subject of much discussion, and the consensus was that they each weighed at least seventy-five pounds. None of us ever got around to putting one on a scale, and their top weight was more like forty pounds, but we liked to think they were heavier. At the first rest period we devoured the cheese sandwiches, and by suppertime we were ready to eat our rifle slings.

The rate of march was two and a half miles per hour, and we would make about fifteen miles per day of steady hiking, keeping to little-traveled roads until we reached the Leon Springs Military Reservation, twenty-five miles north of Fort Sam Houston. The reservation was a spread of rough terrain covering fifty square miles or so of central Texas and consisting mostly of rocks, cactus, scrub oak, and mesquite. It had been a ranch before the army took it over, and the old ranch house, corrals, and watering troughs were still there, falling apart from age and disuse.

There was little motor traffic on the roads we followed, just an occasional rancher or drummer raising dust in a flivver. Our supply wagons were pulled by six-mule teams and followed the foot troops. There was one car in the regiment, a sedan the colonel used in garrison, but when we went into the field he rode a horse.

Pfc. Victor Vogel, 3d Brigade Headquarters Company, at Leon Springs Military Reservation near San Antonio, 1936. *Photograph by the author*

If the entire division was on a training exercise, the horse-drawn artillery was out too. It was a great sight to see a long column of gun carriages and caissons, with six-horse teams perfectly matched for color and size, slick and fit, their coats shining in the sun, leaning into the collars together.

At night we would move off the road and camp wherever we happened to be, pitching two-man pup tents in the best spot we could find. Campsites were easy to find as the country thereabouts was sparsely settled. It was mostly ranch land, on which very little farming was done.

The mission of infantry was "to close with the enemy and destroy or capture him," and this was done by "fire and movement." That is what the book said, and regular army training went by the book. "Fire" was learned on the rifle and automatic weapons ranges. "Movement" was learned in field maneuvers that covered days or weeks, depending on the number of troops involved or the purpose of the training.

There was plenty of "movement," and everyone had a chance to take part in the show. Staff personnel planned the maneuvers, company officers and noncommissioned officers learned tactical operations, and the communications and supply sections worked at their specialties.

For the infantry private, unburdened by responsibility, being in the field was a picnic, an outing to be enjoyed, a carefree excursion into the world of nature. Besides, he didn't have to shine his shoes, pull kitchen police, or stand guard duty. It was hard to beat.

At the start of a field exercise, Company A would spread out in a line of "skirmishers" across a quarter-mile or more of terrain and advance on a distant hill occupied by an "enemy" represented by umpires with colored flags. On the way we would flush deer, armadillos, coyotes, jackrabbits, coveys of quail, and some big diamondback rattlers that were hunting for the rabbits and quail.

There were a lot of stories about those rattlesnakes, their length, how far they could strike, and how fast the venom worked. It was always fatal, according to the reports, and if a man was bitten he was a goner for sure.

One tale was repeated every time we went into the field. A soldier, always in another outfit, was walking down a trail when an eight-foot diamondback uncoiled and struck him between the eyes, killing him before he hit the ground, so quickly did the poison reach his heart. Explaining that a snake could strike only a third of its length, or that if it did strike it would likely be at a leg or ankle and that it was not possible for man to die of snake venom before he fell to the ground would not lay this tale to rest. No one knew the soldier who died, but it was too good a story to give up and was always told to recruits on their first maneuver.

When we reached the hill that was our objective, we would fix the long bayonets we carried to our Springfields and charge to the top, yelling like maniacs and throwing rocks at the umpires if we were certain they couldn't see us. We had nothing against the umpires, but it put a little fun into the show. On top of the hill we planted the company guidon as a symbol of victory and formed squad combat posts to wait for the rolling kitchen to come up with supper.

The rolling kitchen was a big iron stove on wheels that was towed behind the company supply wagon when on the march. The wagon hauled water, rations for the men, feed for the mules, ammunition, tools, tentage, and the company commander's bedroll. The supply sergeant rode on the wagon seat with the mule skinner, and the cooks rode in back with the supplies.

The wagon would catch up with the company about dark and the cooks would prepare supper, usually slumgullion, as beef stew was called, and coffee. Breakfast would be hotcakes, eggs, bacon, and more coffee. That coffee was described as "hot as hell and black as sin," but it sure woke a man up in a hurry.

For lunch we had another cheese sandwich and maybe an orange. Eventually, the army found a substitute for the sandwich in the canned C ration, but it wasn't much of an improvement. My own choice would be the cheese sandwich. Nothing ever took the place of the orange, and the U.S. Army scattered peels all over the world when the war started.

The next day we would have a new objective and we would continue the march through mesquite and cactus, along cow trails or goat paths that began nowhere and led nowhere. Fences were miles apart and then only a couple of strands of barbed wire on flimsy poles stuck in sandy soil by a rancher to mark his boundaries. To cross one the first man placed a stick between the wires to hold them apart while the men of the company stepped through, then the last man kicked out the stick. In a day's march we might see only one or two lonesome cows and a few goats besides the wild animals, but we never saw a human out of uniform.

After supper we cleaned equipment, shaved, and washed as best we could in the limited amount of water we carried. Sometimes we were lucky and found a muddy water hole that would do for a bath if the weather was warm. If it was cold we didn't bother with such foolishness.

When all the high ground in the surrounding country had been captured, we would march back to the regimental base camp and prepare for the next training exercise.

The peak of infantry training was reached in brigade field exercises. The brigade was the largest unit composed solely of infantry and organized for tactical operations in the field. It did not include supporting arms such as artillery or the service branches.

The 3d Infantry Brigade of the 2d Division was made up of two famous army regiments, the 9th and 23d, both with long histories of outstanding service. The 4th Infantry Brigade, with the 1st and 20th regiments, was also assigned to the division but was stationed at Fort Francis E. Warren, Wyoming.

An enlisted man selected for assignment to the brigade headquarters company usually thought himself lucky. The new job took him out of the routine of the line company, gave him a chance to see a broader picture of military training, get a better rating with more pay, and, best of all, ride something. It might be only an escort wagon or a communication cart stringing telephone wire, but it took the load off his feet and the pack off his back. He might even be assigned a horse, one of those half-thoroughbreds the army favored for mounted service, although this could be a disaster if the soldier and the horse did not get on well together. After learning that his seat could get as sore as his feet, a man might change his mind about the new job and wish he were back in a rifle or machine gun company.

The principal mission of the brigade headquarters company was to provide communications with the regiments, and each man was required to learn one or more skills in this department. These could be field telephone systems, radio telegraph, message coding, map reading, horsemanship, or headquarters administration. The radio telephone had not yet been developed for field use, and all communications specialists were trained in Morse code.

One phase of field communications that was not in the book provided some fun when the brigade was in the field at Leon Springs. This plot on the part of enlisted men, usually at night when things were quiet, took advantage of the telephone circuits that were strung from brigade headquarters to the regiments to provide communications between units. The brigade also ran a line back to the base camp switchboard, where it tied into the commercial line and could be connected with the central at Fort Sam Houston to maintain contact with division headquarters.

Any soldier familiar with the system could call back through the field switchboards and reach Fort Sam central, which was operated by a civilian employee. The soldier making the call could ask to be connected with an outside number, and he would be put through to the commercial operator, who would complete the call. It was a sneaky way for a man to check on a wife or girlfriend who thought her soldier would be away for a week or more.

Most soldiers along the line of communications knew each other and were parties to the scheme so there was little chance that a man would be reported for unauthorized use of the telephone line. This may have been classed as one of those acts of misconduct the "Articles of War" warned against, but we didn't worry about it.

Maneuvers did not always come off as planned and could be downright unpleasant, such as the time the 3d Brigade got caught in a big rainstorm, called a "toad strangler" in Texas. I found the weather in the Lone Star State to be more or less satisfactory, if I could forget the hundred-degree temperature and the northers that can drop the temperature forty degrees in a few hours. The rain seemed more dependable. There usually wasn't much of it.

We were at Leon Springs on brigade maneuvers in the spring of 1936 with everything proceeding like a well-oiled military machine was supposed to proceed. The rain started during the first night. It wasn't just an ordinary rain, the kind a man likes to hear when the patter on the pup tent lulls him to sleep and he dreams of the girls in the Texas Star Taxi Dance Hall. This was a downpour that soon became a cloudburst, turning the tents into sieves and blankets into soggy sponges and leaving water standing on the high ground. There was no sleep that night, and the rain continued into the next day, soaking anything that had kept dry overnight. Breakfast was bread and cheese with cold coffee.

When the foot troops moved out that morning the mud clung to their shoes in gobs, and packs soon doubled in weight as they soaked up water. The driving rain blinded the men, and slippery footing slowed the pace, but the march continued through the day.

The second night was no worse than the first; everyone and everything had absorbed all the water possible. Tents were pitched, and although they afforded little protection from water they gave some shelter from the chilling wind. From time to time the downpour slackened, but only for short periods, then it would come again, with no break in the clouds.

Around noon of the third day, with the rain still falling and the men plodding through the maneuver with no enthusiasm for the job, Brig. Gen. A. T. Ovenshine, the brigade commander, called a halt and ordered everyone back to Fort Sam Houston.

Pvt. Bill Maitland, writing about this event for the 2d Division newspaper, the *Indianhead*, reported that men of the

3d Brigade spent three days in the rain chasing through the cactus and mesquite like hounds after jackrabbits. General Ovenshine did not see the humor in this journalism and called Maitland to his office. After explaining the purpose of field maneuvers and why this training should not be taken lightly, the general terminated Bill's career as a reporter. Still, Bill had a point—we did spend a lot of time chasing across Texas.

The assistant division commander of the 2d Division in 1939–40 was Brig. Gen. Joseph W. Stilwell, better known to the troops as "Vinegar Joe" and later famous for his campaigns as commander of the China-Burma-India theater of operations. He had a reputation for being impatient and short-tempered, but he was popular with enlisted men because he was never too busy to pass the time of day with them in the field. It was common to hear a soldier tell his buddies, "I talked to Vinegar Joe this morning. He asked me how things were going in the outfit." Maybe that was all that was said, but it was a great morale builder for the man and he would never forget it.

In the field General Stilwell set the example of leadership for officers and enlisted men to follow. He slept in a pup tent along with the rest of us and at dawn would jump out of the blankets and shadow box vigorously for five or ten minutes. At this time he was in his fifties, trim and fit.

February, 1940, found the 2d Division on a field exercise in South Texas, somewhere between Fowlerton and Three Rivers. This was the winter of the big snow, one that native Texans still remember, and the weather was unusually cold. Whenever we took a break or camped for the night, we would build a fire of mesquite wood. On one occasion several of us were sitting around a fire, shooting the bull, when Vinegar Joe walked up. We jumped to our feet and snapped a salute. He snapped one back and said, "Make room, men." Then he squatted on his heels, holding his hands to the heat, squinting through the smoke from under the curled brim of the campaign hat he always wore. He sat there for a time, asking how things were going and commenting on the weather, then jumped up and bounced off through the mesquite.

During this training, Gen. George Marshall visited the 2d Division. He had been appointed chief of staff of the army and was inspecting troops in the field. Maybe the brass in Washington suspected that something big was going to break, for the Russians and Finns were at war, but if so they didn't bother to pass it down to the lower ranks.

The commander of the 2d Division was Maj. Gen. Walter Krueger, an entirely different type of officer from Stilwell. Krueger had been an enlisted man in the army during the Spanish-American War and was later commissioned. He was a big man, dignified in bearing and appearance. Though he was known as a strict commander, he was well liked by the men of the division. During World War II he commanded the 6th Army in the Pacific theater of operations under General MacArthur.

The purpose of field training was to acquaint officers and soldiers with tactical operations, communications, and supply procedures and to experience the hardships of living in the open, but it fell far short of teaching a man what it was like to face an enemy.

CHAPTER FOUR

The Firing Range

The Springfield 30.06 ("thirty-ought-six") bolt-action, clip-fed rifle was the finest infantry weapon known to man and was the biggest source of military training, hard work, and sport the regular army knew. It was also the means by which a soldier could earn extra pay because qualification on the firing range as an expert rifleman paid five dollars a month, and a sharpshooter received three dollars monthly when the money was available. During the hard times of the 1930s, when funds were scarce, only experts received the bonanza, which made competition keener. Five dollars could amount to 25 percent of a private's pay and bought a lot of beer and Bull Durham tobacco.

Rifle training was serious business, and we worked at it for several months each year. In early spring, while the regiment was still in barracks, we would begin preliminary training in sighting, positions, trigger squeeze, and other basic principles of marksmanship. The positions were standing, or offhand as we called it, sitting, kneeling, and prone, all using the rifle sling for support. The sling, a leather strap attached to the rifle for carrying the piece, was a necessary aid for accurate shooting.

Standing, sitting, and kneeling positions were used at distances of two hundred and three hundred yards, both for slow and rapid fire. The prone position was used at five hundred yards. Five hundred yards is more than a quarter-

Men of the 3d Brigade at the rifle range, Leon Springs Military Reservation, 1936. *Photograph by the author*

mile, and hitting a bull's-eye twenty inches in diameter required a keen eye and a steady hand. Within the bull's-eye was another circle, the V-ring, half the diameter of the bull, and an expert rifleman was expected to put at least half his shots in the smaller area.

But the sporting test came at two hundred yards, firing offhand at an eight-inch bull's-eye. A record course was ten shots, with no time limit, although five minutes was ample and experienced shooters fired faster, using a rhythmic cadence that grouped the hits within a small area.

It was the trigger squeeze that separated the squirrel hunters from the scattergun shooters. Most of the technique of marksmanship could be learned, but a man had to have the "feel" of the trigger to be an expert rifleman. The secret of proper squeeze lay in finding the slack, which was in the

trigger of every Springfield. This slack, an almost impercep-
tible movement of the trigger, could be determined only by
feel.

When the slack was taken up by the finger, a steady pressure
was held on the trigger while the sights were aligned on the
bull's-eye. The trigger was squeezed while the sights were in
proper alignment, and when the "bull" wavered off the front
sight the pressure on the trigger was again held. If the trigger
was squeezed properly, the shot went off with the bull resting
on the front sight without the shooter knowing the exact
moment of firing. This would result in a good hit, a five or a
four, but if the shooter flinched, or jerked the trigger, he would
be lucky to hit the target where he could score a three or a two.

Scoring was five points for a bull's-eye, then four and three
in the next outer rings, with any hit on the scoring surface
outside the three rings being a two. There was no score of one.
Forty was a good offhand score, and few shooters could top
of forty-five. A perfect score of fifty at this range was rare.

After several weeks of work on the basic principles we fired
small-caliber weapons on the indoor range to perfect positions
and sharpen shooting eyes. This practice conditioned men for
the grueling test on the outdoor ranges, where we could be
shooting for the money.

In late spring the regiment would move to Camp Bullis,
twenty-five miles north of Fort Sam Houston, where the firing
ranges were located. There we spent a month in tents while
conducting field training and range firing.

Once firing began, nothing was left to chance. Each man
had a coach when shooting for practice, even though he was
an expert. Units bought spotting telescopes to observe each
shot as it was marked on the target. Micrometer gauges were
used to set sights to minute fractions. Sighting mirrors were
attached to barrels so the coaches could see the sight alignment and advise the shooter of any error. Special shooting
coats and gloves were bought or made by each man. These
coats were padded with sheepskin at shoulder, elbow, and

biceps to relieve strain and could cost as much as a month's pay. Field telephones connected firing line with target butts to give instructions to pit crews and to keep shooters advised of such details as wind variation, shadows, dust, or other sophisticated problems, real or imagined, that might influence a man's performance.

Some soldiers provided their own Springfields. This was possible under a regulation that enabled an officer or enlisted man to buy a firearm from the Ordnance Department. An arsenal was located at San Antonio, and such purchase was a common practice for it ensured that a soldier would have a weapon he could depend on for record firing.

Rifles bought from the arsenal were always "star-gauged," that is, marked with a small star stamped in the barrel just below the front sight. The star indicated that the rifle bore was accurate to 1/100 of an inch, had no mechanical flaws, and could be depended on to place a bullet exactly where aimed.

Pfc. George Odell of Headquarters Company, 3d Infantry Brigade, owned one of these star-gauged Springfields. George was a professional soldier if one ever put on a uniform, and we would kid him about having a U.S. branded on his buttocks. In 1936 George had more than twelve years in the army, was a bugler, telephone lineman, and radio telegraph operator, could drive a team of mules, and was an expert with rifle and pistol. George had been a corporal in a rifle company but had changed outfits and lost his rank. This didn't bother him because he was happy anywhere in the army, liked to move around, and never served more than one enlistment in the same company. He had been an actor, too, having had a part in the movie *Wings* as a German soldier.

When George transferred to our outfit he didn't like the rifle that was issued to him so he went to the San Antonio arsenal and bought one. The price was about thirty-five dollars, his month's pay. It paid off, for he fired the best score in the company.

Before firing for record, each man would fire the course two

31

or three times for practice. This gave him a chance to sight in his rifle, get the feel of it, perfect his timing, and get used to the beating he took from the Springfield. All firing data were noted in the range book each soldier kept and to which he referred before firing a course.

The regular army did not keep records of casualties inflicted on shooters by their own weapons, but these occurred in large numbers. Hardly a man left the firing line without a black eye, a bloody nose, a bruised cheek, a fractured jaw, or busted teeth. The Springfield packed tremendous power, propelling a bullet with a muzzle velocity of more then 2,800 feet per second, and the recoil would punish a man unmercifully. Many a recruit would close his eyes, grit his teeth, and jerk the trigger, dreading the impact that followed, suffering in silence until the got the hang of it through practice and proper coaching. The way to prevent injury lay in proper position and sling adjustment, which took up most of the recoil. Still, many an expert walked off the firing line with a sore jaw.

In modern automatic rifles the action of the weapon absorbs the recoil and eliminates this shock, thus eliminating injury to the shooter. But the Springfield required discipline, and it built character.

Shooting for record was the final test, for those scores went in the books and determined whether a man drew the coveted extra fiver each month for the next year. There were no excuses and no second chances. Only if something went wrong on the range that was not the fault of the shooter was he entitled to an "alibi" round, a reprieve granted only by the range officer. This was the big day, the day we hoped would dawn bright and clear, with no wind.

Wind was an important factor in marksmanship, for it could change the trajectory of a bullet. Correct estimation of wind speed and direction was necessary to compensate for this variation and was carefully calculated. Old-timers could "read" the wind, and their advice was closely followed.

All this had to be learned and practiced before firing for

record, for when a man was called to the line for the final test he was on his own—no coaching, no help, no advice. He had to depend on his own knowledge, experience, and the notes he had jotted in his range book.

When it was over, a man had a feeling of relief, even if he had not shot as well as he had hoped or knew that he could when at his best. He didn't have to take that beating from the Springfield anymore and could relax from the emotional strain of competition. His score went into his personal record for another year, and he drew extra pay if he had earned it.

Then, if he had not already served his turn in the target pits, he had his chance at that unforgettable experience. Working targets was a challenge. If swinging a sledge on a rock pile, manning an oar in a slave galley, and shoveling concrete were lumped together it would give the general idea of pulling targets in Texas on a hot day.

Each target point consisted of two frames, six by six feet, that ran up and down on cables so as to balance each other. This was the theory, but they never did, and the operator had to put his back into them with every shot fired. The target would be run down, the shot scored, the target run back up for the next shot, and the score signaled to the firing line. The operator stripped to the waist, would hoist and lower those targets from early morning to late afternoon.

It was fascinating in one way. There would be a snap overhead as the .30-caliber bullet passed through the target at about three times the speed of sound and the operator would haul down the frame. As the target reached bottom, the rifle report would be heard from the firing point because the sound traveled much slower than the ball.

A soldier could be attacked by those targets if he wasn't careful. If he hoisted the rear frame instead of pulling down on the front one, the descending target would strike a blow on his head that would make him lose all interest in target pulling. Sooner or later this happened to everyone in the pits, for as the day wore on the frames became heavier with each pull and it

33

was easy to forget whether they traveled up or down.

When the hard part was over we fired the heavy machine gun, the Browning automatic rifle, and the pistol to become familiar with all infantry weapons. Running the bayonet course and the use of hand and rifle grenades were also part of the training program, but they were not as exacting or as challenging as the Springfield.

The Colt .45-caliber pistol came close for it was a sporting weapon and fun to shoot. It could be dangerous to friend and foe alike, however, and it was easy to lose a toe or shoot a buddy in the rear end, which did not build confidence in the rest of the outfit.

The pistol was an accurate weapon in the hands of an expert, but few men learned to shoot it well because it was not balanced properly and was hard to hold on the target. It took a lot of practice to make a man a good shot with the pistol. It was seldom used in combat, but to have it handy gave a man a feeling of security.

Besides participating in regular gunnery practice, the machine gun companies, of which there were three in an infantry regiment, took part in the Clark Trophy test on an armywide basis. This event was named for Edwin Howard Clark, the originator of the idea.

Clark graduated from the United States Military Academy in 1917 and served with the 1st Machine Gun Battalion, 1st Division, in World War I. In 1920 he was retired for disability in line of duty with the rank of captain, and he died in Baltimore, Maryland, on July 29, 1923. In his will Captain Clark established a trust fund to provide a trophy and cash prizes for the purpose of stimulating interest in machine gunnery. Competition was to be conducted under the direction of the War Department, and the award was to be known as the Machine Gunner's Trophy, but it was usually called the Clark Trophy.

The chief of infantry—an office no longer in existence— drew up rules for the test, and first competition was held in

1927. It was based on the average score of the company in regular gunnery practice, and the winner was Company D, 28th Infantry Regiment.

Later the scoring was expanded to include not only gunnery and marksmanship but basic training, a road march, making camp, and a field inspection. The march covered fifteen miles and was made on foot with mule-drawn gun carriages. It was to be completed in precisely six hours, a faster or slower time counting against the total score. Fifteen miles meant exactly that, no more, no less.

During one of the Clark tests, Maj. P. W. Clarkson, executive officer of the 3d Infantry Brigade, was head of the examining board. He instructed me to lay out a course for the fifteen-mile march and indicated on a map the route to be followed.

"Yes, sir," I said. "I'll get a car from the motor pool and check it with the speedometer."

"You will not," said the major. "Get someone to help you and measure the exact distance with a hundred-foot tape. Not one inch more or less."

That is the way another soldier and I did it. We spent two days laying the tape down and picking it up, but when we finished we knew the job had been done right. It was a good lesson in how to be precise.

P. W. Clarkson was one of the finest gentlemen anyone could ever know. He had been a machine gun officer in Europe during World War I and had served as professor of mathematics at West Point. He was a big man, with a forthright and pleasant manner that soldiers liked. He became a major general in World War II and was in charge of the atomic tests held at Bikini Island in the Pacific in July, 1946.

The Clark Trophy test generated keen competition and became an important event in the annual training schedule of machine gun companies. Not only was it an honor to win the trophy, but the prize money was an added incentive. Money went to the first-, second-, and third-place finishers and could amount to several hundred dollars, based on the return of the trust fund investments. The amounts were substantial in those days, considering the purchasing power of the dollar.

Rivalry became so fierce that some units were accused of padding scores and placing recruits on special duty so they would not show up poorly. Mules, which pulled the gun carriages, were brought to the peak of condition for the march so they could cross the finish line in the time required. Past tests were studied and inspections rehearsed. With prestige and money at stake, nothing was left to chance.

In 1937 the competition was discontinued because of the difficulty in drawing up a test that would meet all conditions on a fair basis. There was also a great amount of detail required by examining boards in scoring, which resulted in an undesirable delay in announcing the winner.

Company D, 65th Infantry, was the last winner, but the outfit didn't get to keep the trophy, a bronze casting of three soldiers manning a machine gun. When the competition ended, it was called in by the War Department and at last report was stored in a supply depot in Virginia.

Efforts have been made to renew interest in the event under modern conditions, but nothing has come of them. Perhaps it is because the army no longer has mules.

CHAPTER FIVE

The Outfit

The infantry company, cavalry troop, or artillery battery was the smallest unit with both tactical and administrative capabilities and duties. It was able to fight on its own resources for a limited time and could handle the necessary business of supply and personnel management. To the enlisted soldier it was "the outfit," and he seldom called it anything else.

The outfit provided everything a man needed—food, clothing, shelter, and security from the outside world, where no one was in charge. On the last day of each month, the outfit paid a soldier enough to keep him in Bull Durham tobacco, buy a few beers, and make a trip to town if that was what he wanted.

In return, the soldier was required to be present most of the time, carry out orders given him in a reasonably efficient manner without too much complaining, and do nothing to disgrace the uniform or the outfit. The last requirement was the most important.

The boss of the outfit was the "Old Man," officially the commanding officer, usually a captain or a first lieutenant with considerable service behind him. Sometimes he was a new second lieutenant just out of the military academy at West Point on his first assignment. In that case, the pink-cheeked, beardless youth was still the Old Man, but primarily he was an observer learning the ways of the regulars while the first sergeant kept the outfit running.

Occasionally the Old Man was a captain in his forties, maybe even fifties, sweating out enough service for retirement, at the end of the line, militarily speaking. This was the result of a lenient policy that rewarded past service, usually in World War I, and allowed an officer to leave the army with honor and retirement pay.

Because of the limited number of officers, there was usually only one commissioned rank in the outfit. If there were two, the second one was probably one of the new second looies just out of West Point. An officer might be in command of two outfits at the same time, when the commander of one was absent, since an officer was always required to be on hand.

Next in the chain of command was the first sergeant, also called the "first soldier," the "topkick," or merely the "top." He was the ramrod of the outfit, the man who kept it running. Most likely he was a veteran of World War I or the Mexican border campaign, but sometimes he went back as far as the Philippine insurrection. When the commanding officer was absent, the topkick had full responsibility until the Old Man returned.

The platoon sergeants were on the next lower rung of the ladder, responsible for the performance of the squads assigned to their platoons. They saw that the training progressed according to the schedule and that discipline was maintained. Most had five or six enlistments, or more, in the army.

The outfit also had a mess sergeant, a supply sergeant, and a clerk who were responsible for their special departments and reported directly to the first sergeant.

The corporals, lowest of the noncommissioned ranks, were squad leaders, in charge of the smallest tactical units of the military machine. A corporal was the leader in direct contact with the privates of his squad and responsible for their conduct and performance of duty. He might have two or three enlistments behind him, or he could be nearing retirement with thirty years of service on his record.

Privates were a diverse lot. There were recruits on their first enlistment learning the basics of soldiering. Some had enough after one enlistment and left to look for a job on the outside;

many re-upped and made it a career. There were old-timers who had knocked around the army, the navy, and the marine corps, enlisting in one branch, then another, as the mood suited them. Unable to take the responsibility that went with higher rank, or not wanting it, these men served out their time because it was the only life they knew or wanted.

Privates also fell into the category of the smart soldier who liked the service and made it his career and who could be relied on to do his duty well, take responsibility, and prepare for advancement. When a vacancy in the noncommissioned ranks occurred, he was considered for promotion. Some of these men had enlisted for West Point preparatory school, failed to make the grades necessary for entry into the academy, and chose to remain in the army. Others had been to private military schools, tried the army, and found it little different so they stayed.

Outfits were small, seldom more than ninety men at full strength, and the men were close because of the barracks life. They knew each others' qualifications, temperaments, and sense of humor or lack of it. There were no secrets, and if a man tried to hide something he was suspect. Sometimes a "bolshevik" would show up, transferring in from another outfit that wanted to get rid of him. A bolshevik couldn't get along with anyone and didn't fit anywhere, and a way was found to discharge him as soon as possible.

The closeness of the outfit promoted good relationships and mutual respect, for all had much in common. Their lives were open books because they had nothing to be ashamed of. Everything was known about every man and was in the record, a small pamphlet on file in the orderly room of the outfit under the care of the first sergeant and company clerk.

Company A, 9th Infantry, was a good outfit, running smoothly, like a well-oiled machine, with little friction between its parts, which were the men. It was a friendly, good-humored group, professional, reliable, dedicated to the military service. But it was no different from many regular outfits.

First Sergeant Moree was the topkick of Company A. He was a veteran of World War I and one of the few men ever to take a bayonet through the chest and live to tell about it. In the bull sessions in the barracks, Moree would take off his shirt and show the scar to the new men. It was part of recruit training to see Moree's scar and listen to his tales of hand-to-hand combat in 1918.

Company A took pride in its record of rifle marksmanship, for an outfit was expected to qualify 100 percent of its members as marksmen, sharpshooters, or experts on the rifle range. A man who could not score high enough to qualify with a least a rating of marksman was a "bolo" and considered a disgrace to the regulars. The term bolo originated in the Philippine insurrection, when the heavy, long knife was commonly used by the Moros. If a man could not shoot well he could always use a bolo.

Some men had difficulty with the firing positions or could not readily grasp the mechanics of being a good shot. These men got extra help from noncoms and buddies, who coached them until they got the hang of shooting properly. They were encouraged to give that extra effort which enabled them to make a qualifying score. Company A had no bolos.

Headquarters Company, 3d Brigade, was another good outfit. The men were picked from the two regiments of the brigade, the 9th and 23d, for their good character, reliability, and potential to learn new duties.

In the field the mission of brigade headquarters company was to provide communications to the regiments and to division headquarters and to perform administrative duties required by the brigade commander and his staff. In garrison the training schedule was designed to improve the skills of each man in his specialty.

The brigade headquarters company consisted of a radio section, a field telephone section, a message center, a headquarters section, a transportation section, and a supply section. Each man could work in at least two of these sections. All men had completed basic training in a rifle or machine gun company and were well grounded in the organization of the brigade.

The brigade commander was a brigadier general, with a staff consisting of an executive officer, a major; an S-1, administration and personnel; S-2, military intelligence; S-3, operations and training; and an S-4, logistics. The S-2 and S-3 were combined, due to the shortage of officers available for this duty. The brigade commander also had an aide-de-camp, a lieutenant.

The enlisted section of brigade headquarters included the sergeant major, a topographical draftsman, and two administrative clerks.

The two regiments of the brigade, the 9th and 23d, were identical in organization, each consisting of three battalions, a headquarters company and a service company. Each battalion was made up of three rifle companies and a machine gun company. The companies were lettered from A to M, with the J being omitted. The reason for this omission seems to have become clouded by time, although explanations having to do with phonetic objections to the letter J seem probable.

Each regimental commander, a colonel, was served by a staff, which was organized the same as the brigade staff. The regimental commander did not rate an aide-de-camp.

There were no medical personnel assigned to the brigade. Regimental aid stations were manned by medical detachments from division, and sick or injured men were sent directly to the Fort Sam Houston hospital from the aid stations.

Regimental headquarters company furnished personnel for the administrative staff of the regiment, communications, and a weapons platoon armed with mortars and anti-tank guns.

Service Company furnished transportation for the regiment, which prior to the adoption of motor vehicles in 1935 was mule drawn.

A battalion was often commanded by a major, although the Table of Organization authorized a lieutenant colonel for the position. The battalion was also entitled to a staff the same as the regiment, but in most cases it would likely be a patchwork of personnel drawn from the companies for a specific training exercise.

Total strength of the brigade, including the two regiments, was approximately 2,500 officers and enlisted men.

Men of an outfit would stick together off duty as well as on and especially if a comrade had been roughed up by civilians. A good demonstration of this was made by an artillery battery at Fort Sam when one of its men was thrown out of a westside honkytonk in San Antonio after spending all his pay. The following Saturday night twenty or so gunners, in civilian clothes, strolled into the joint by twos and threes and ordered beer. They sat around for a time, drinking and dancing with the girls as though it was just another beer party. Then, at a signal from one of the soldiers, they quickly smashed chairs, tables, and fixtures, tossing the splintered furniture in a pile on a dance floor. In a matter of minutes the destruction was completed and the artillerymen departed, disappearing into the crowd on the street before the police arrived. Although the owner of the bar suspected who was behind the fracas, he kept it to himself, knowing the soldiers would stick together and he stood little chance of collecting damages.

But there was more to this esprit de corps than just being a member of an organization. Most outfits had long histories of military service, and a man felt he was part of that, too. Most soldiers couldn't explain it, or never tried, but they were proud of it.

A roster of officers and enlisted men assigned to 3d Brigade Headquarters and Headquarters Company from July, 1934, to October, 1939, has been reconstructed from records, photographs, and my memory. The officers and enlisted men whose names appear were assigned at some time during this period, and many of the enlisted men served for the entire period. This roster is included as Appendix A.

The Lineage and Honors of the 3d Brigade, an official record of the Department of the Army, shows that it took part in six campaigns in Europe during World War I. The 4th Brigade, assigned to the 2d Division during World I, was composed of marine corps regiments and not army units.

The 9th and 23d infantry regiments are not included in the brigade honors because they have their own lineage.

The 3d Brigade was disbanded October 3, 1939, due to the reorganization of the infantry division. It was reactivated January 25, 1963, and again assigned to the 2d Division and stationed in Korea, facing the communist forces along the 38th Parallel.

The number of officers and enlisted men of Headquarters and Headquarters Company, 3d Infantry Brigade, who rose to high rank, commissioned and noncommissioned, was remarkable when considering the small number assigned to the outfit. Seldom were more than half a dozen officers and forty-five enlisted men of all ranks assigned at any one time.

Five officers of the rank of major and below became general officers, and eleven enlisted men were later commissioned. It is impossible to determine the number of enlisted men who served as warrant officers or noncommissioned officers during World War II and after, but the number was significant.

This outstanding contribution to the leadership of the wartime army by the brigade headquarters and headquarters company can be attributed to the system of selecting personnel, the training program, and the characteristically high level of morale. When there was a need for highly qualified leaders, the outfit did more than its share in meeting the demand.

The regiments of the brigade, the 9th and 23d, likewise had outstanding records in this respect. Many enlisted men of those regiments later served as commissioned officers and stepped up to be leaders of companies and battalions. In Europe and Japan, as well as in the United States, I often met officers I had known back at Fort Sam Houston when we were enlisted men in the 3d Brigade.

The regiments of the brigade were identical in organization, each consisting of a commander, a colonel, with his staff, a headquarters company to provide administrative and communication personnel, a service company to handle supplies, and three combat battalions. Each battalion consisted of a commander, usually a major, with a small staff, three rifle companies, and one machine gun company. Communication and supply personnel for the battalions were furnished by regimental headquarters and service companies.

CHAPTER SIX

The Old Man

The commanding officer of a company, troop or battery was always called the Old Man, never to his face, to be sure, but always when mentioned among themselves by the enlisted men of an outfit. No disrespect was meant; it was like an honorary title.

There was no pattern for an Old Man, just as there was no pattern for a soldier, and they came in a variety of sizes, degrees of ability, and backgrounds. Some came from the ranks in World War I, many were graduates of the United States Military Academy, and a scattering came from the Reserve Officer Training Corps of universities. Some were able with a bright future and in World War II were promoted rapidly in command or staff positions. Others were incompetent, drifting along until retirement or until they were eased out of the army in one way or another. Most got the job done in a satisfactory manner, stayed with the outfit for two or three years, and then went to a new assignment and were forgotten by the soldiers in the company.

Now and then an Old Man came along who stood above the others, knew the job better, worked at it harder, and got better results. He would be an officer who insisted on high standards of conduct and performance, was firm, but at the same time could overlook a mistake, an Old Man who was concerned with the welfare of the enlisted men in the outfit and set an example of leadership for the soldiers he led. Not all officers had these qualities. Some were seldom with the company except when they were required to be there for a duty that could not be delegated to a noncommissioned officer. Others remained aloof from the men, even when with the outfit, as if they were uncomfortable about enlisted soldiers. At the other extreme, an officer who was overly friendly made soldiers feel uncomfortable. There was a line between commissioned and enlisted in the old army, but in most cases both knew where to draw it.

The good officer, the best leader, found the middle ground, where he had the respect of the men and returned their loyalty. The commanding officer of Headquarters Company, 3d Brigade, in 1933–34 fit this description.

First Lt. W. E. Dunkleberg was in his thirties at the time, for promotion was slow and a lieutenant might make captain by the time he was forty, then stay in that rank for years. Majors were often in their fifties. Dunkleberg was tall and trim with an easy manner, but he demanded a high standard of performance and professionalism from the men in the company. Soldiers respected him and knew they would be treated fairly.

There was little talk of a real shooting war in those days, and most men gave little indication that they ever thought about it. Although we were trained for war, the actual possibility seemed remote. In this respect this Old Man was different too.

The company had turned out for a full field inspection and after the formalities were out of the way Lieutenant Dunkleberg gave us a brief talk on the mission of the army and the part we would play if war came. His closing words went something like this: "One of these days we may be called on to pack our equipment and move out to defend our country. We don't know where we might go or when we will get back. When that time comes we will be expected to do the job we have been trained to do. Some of us will have to take a great deal more responsibility than we ever had. It is up to us to be ready."

No other officer had ever mentioned the subject to us, and

the men of the company never discussed the matter, but the Old Man's words turned out to be prophetic. It is not likely that he had intended to foretell the future with such accuracy, but that is the way it turned out. Before the Japanese struck at Pearl Harbor and World War II had been declared, the brigade headquarters company had been disbanded and the men scattered to other outfits. Frequently I would run into one of them at a distant station, and many had indeed taken on more responsibility as officers, warrant officers, or senior noncommissioned officers.

The Old Man moved up the ladder too—he was promoted to brigadier general.

CHAPTER SEVEN

Last Stable Call

Long after the motor vehicle became commonplace in America the military services continued to use horses and mules, and World War II still found some army units depending on animals for transportation. Maybe it was because of economy, or simply reluctance to change, or maybe because of sentiment, but it took a long time to replace the stables with motor pools, and the horse soldier died hard.

Even the infantry, the branch of service remembered most for blisters on the feet, carried animals on the rosters of headquarters, service, and machine gun companies. Each animal was listed on the morning report by name and number, the same as their human comrades, and they were entitled to good rations, suitable quarters, and medical treatment as were other members of the army.

Each had its own personality, too. Some were dependable and could be relied on to do their duty at all times. Others didn't take military service seriously and would clown around, stealing gloves, pipes, and miscellaneous articles from the pockets of unsuspecting soldiers or hiding grooming tools in the hay, just for mischief. Then there were the outlaws, those with a reputation for being unmanageable and were not to be trusted.

There was one four-legged member of the 3d Brigade Headquarters mounted section that literally left its imprint on numerous soldiers. His name was Ted Harley, and undoubt-

75-mm gun section, Field Artillery, ca. 1934. *Courtesy National Archives*

edly he was the most independent critter that ever wore the brand of the U.S. Army. At least, there is no record of any other horse trotting forward to claim the distinction.

Ted Harley was a handsome bay gelding with a white stripe down his nose and big, brown eyes that he would roll backward to see what was behind him. If it was something he didn't like, he would kick it, or bite it, or try to buck it off, or run away from it—either one at a time or all at once, whichever suited him at the moment.

In the infantry, horses were used as officers' mounts, in messenger service, or as polo ponies. Polo was a popular sport in the army, and every horse was a prospect for the game if fast enough and shifty enough.

Ted Harley was both fast and shifty; in fact, no other horse could come close to him in the latter department, but he was also unpredictable, which eliminated him as a polo mount. He had his chance more than once, for there was always an optimistic polo player who would look Ted Harley over, note his fine conformation, intelligent head, and sound condition, and then try him out in a practice game. That was as far as he ever got, for Ted Harley had his own opinion of polo as he did of everything else. He didn't like it.

Sometimes he would start out all right, playing the game in a sportsmanlike manner, but this was just to build up confidence in his rider and lull him into a careless moment. Then Ted Harley would suddenly change direction on the field and head for the nearest exit at a run, leaving the rider flat on his back in the middle of a stampede. Or, if he took a notion to follow the ball, he would run over everything in his way, which is not the best manners in the game.

Nor did Ted Harley meet the requirements of an officer's mount because respect for rank meant nothing to him. Enlisted or commissioned, he played no favorites; he treated everybody the same—rough.

That left only one career open to Ted Harley, that of messenger's mount, and because messengers were always privates, there was no way for them to get out of the job. Somebody had to team up with Ted Harley. And that is how I became acquainted with him.

We were both assigned to Headquarters Company, 3d Infantry Brigade, and, though Ted Harley had more service, we were equal in rank and neither was entitled to any privilege over the other. It soon became apparent that the horse took a different view of this for he pulled rank on me from the start.

Sgt. Louis Loucks was in charge of the headquarters mounted section and responsible for horsemanship training. Louis was a fine man, a veteran regular, and a father-adviser to young soldiers in the outfit. (Ironically, he was run over and killed by a truck after the infantry was motorized.)

"Had any experience with horses?" Loucks asked when I reported to the stable for the first time.

"I'm a riding fool," I bragged, stretching the truth a little.

Actually, my horsemanship was limited to riding Old Maud

around the farm when I was a small boy, but it wouldn't have made any difference for there was only one horse unattended at the picket line and I was the only man without a horse.

"Ted Harley is your mount," Loucks announced, pointing to the lonesome bay. "Saddle up."

I knew where the saddle and bridle went and how to attach them to the animal so there wasn't any problem up to that point. The horse stood quietly while I placed the bits in his mount and cinched down the McClellan.

"Stand to horse," shouted Sergeant Loucks.

In this position the horseman stood at attention to the left of his horse's head, right hand holding the reins just below the animal's jaw. Without moving his head, Ted Harley sized me up with his left eye.

"Prepare to mount," Loucks yelled.

At this command the reins were looped over the horse's head, taken up short, and gripped by the left hand along with a fistful of mane to hold on to. Then, doing a right-face, the rider twisted the left stirrup forward and placed the left foot therein, leaving the seat of the pants stuck out in an exposed and vulnerable position.

"Mount, " bellowed Loucks.

The other riders swung into their saddles, and I started to do the same but didn't make it. At the command, Ted Harley turned his head and struck with the lightning speed of a rattlesnake at my posterior, connecting with a powerful blow that knocked me flat. Lying on the ground, I expected to be dispatched by a kick in the head, but I was safe enough, for Ted Harley was not homicidal by nature and he wanted to save me for more fun in the future.

"Get up and get on that horse. The rest of you sit at attention. Wipe off those grins," Loucks ordered the section in one breath. On a docile gelding named Whitey, Louis Loucks looked like one of those pictures of Napoleon at Waterloo in history books.

Even the horses listened when Louis Loucks gave orders,

and while Ted Harley was momentarily diverted I scrambled into the saddle as the sergeant yelled, "Right by twos—ho," and the section rode off for drill.

Five days each week mounted personnel went through exercises, Saturday being reserved for inspection and Sunday a day off, and each morning brought a new experience full of excitement as Ted Harley displayed his talent for doing the unexpected. That horse must have stayed awake at night thinking up new tricks to try the next day, for it was impossible to guess what he would do next.

The morning after my first encounter with Ted Harley (in which the horse was the undisputed winner) the section reported to stables on schedule, and although there was a sore spot in the vicinity of my left rear pocket I was ready to try again. This time I tied Ted Harley up short on the picket line so he couldn't use his teeth, laid the saddle blanket on the prescribed area between withers and croup, and swung the saddle in place. At the instant of impact Ted Harley gave a mighty buck which sent saddle and blanket flying over his head to strike another horse, causing it to rear in panic. The entire picket line turned into a swirling storm of dust while Sergeant Loucks bawled for men and horses to come to attention.

After some delay, discipline won over disorder, I got the saddle on Ted Harley, the section returned to sanity, and we rode off like the book said—in a military manner.

There were days when Ted Harley would do his job like anybody else in the outfit and was a credit to the service. He was an excellent mount when he worked at it and when on his good behavior would respond to the lightest touch of rein or leg, would change leads properly, and do all exercises at the walk, trot, or canter without a fault. Nevertheless, there was always the possibility that Ted Harley was lulling the rider into a false sense of security so he could spring a surprise on him.

Everyone who knew everything about horses, or thought he did, tried to explain Ted Harley's behavior, but none of the explanations made much sense. It wasn't his health because he was sound of wind and limb and his coat glistened like a pair of garrison shoes on Saturday morning. He cleaned up all the oats and hay he could get and never tired under the saddle so it wasn't a physical problem. It wasn't poor treatment either, for Ted Harley got everything he was entitled to by the regulations and wasn't required to pull any duty other members of the outfit were not called on to perform, so he had no complaint there. It could have been that he just didn't like army routine and discipline. There were some soldiers like that and it could have been the same with horses. He might have been just a little bit bolshevik.

The horse show was a popular form of entertainment on posts such as Fort Sam Houston where there were enough animals to provide good competition. Mules as well as horses took part, and one of the exciting events on a program was the wagon race. Each entry, a supply wagon pulled by a six-mule team, with driver and his assistant on the box, would careen around the course in a cloud of dust, racing against the clock because the size of the show ring did not permit more than one entry at a time.

Entries in these shows had the enthusiastic support of the men of their outfits, and mounts and riders were cheered wildly by comrades and jeered unmercifully by men of rival units. It was not uncommon for soldiers to resort to fisticuffs to settle differences of opinion concerning the ability of their favorites. Nor was the decision of the ring judge always received with approval by soldiers in the crowd, military courtesy and customs of the service to the contrary.

At one Fort Sam Houston show, the ladies' three-gaited class was dominated by two outstanding riders, one the wife of a captain, the other a sergeant's wife. The sergeant's wife put her horse through its paces with reckless confidence that completely won the already prejudiced soldiers, who applauded her every move in the ring. The captain's wife, though a competent rider, received only silence as she left the arena.

Typical supply wagon and six-mule team used by army units until 1935.
Courtesy National Archives

After the two contestants had been called back to repeat the required movements on their mounts, the judge declared the captain's wife the winner of the class. The disgruntled soldiers, who had already picked the sergeant's wife as the winner, whistled, shouted, and stomped the bleacher seats in disgust until the judge, an officer of the post, ordered silence and threatened to stop the show. He then explained to the crowd that his decision was based on points of performance by both rider and horse, which quieted the soldiers but did not change their opinion.

Horses filled the more glamorous jobs, and the hard work of pulling the wheeled transport was done by mules, with the exception of artillery gun teams, which were made up of horses. A six-mule team with a driver and assistant driver was hitched to a supply wagon to haul supplies to the line company it supported. All wagons of the regiment were assigned to

Service Company and would operate as a "train" until dispersed, when each wagon would join its company. When the regimental train was on the road in column, with canvas canopies in place, it was a picture of the Old West come alive.

The machine gun cart, a small carriage with wire-spoked wheels, was pulled by one mule attended by a "mule leader." The mule leader had an assistant who followed behind the animal in case help was needed at that end. The job of assistant mule leader was low on the scale of military prestige and normally filled by a man on his first enlistment.

Another wheeled vehicle that was mule-powered was the K-cart, a device that carried a large roll of field telephone wire to be laid on the ground over long distances. Why it was called a K-cart was unknown to the soldiers who manned it, but it could have been because it was a killer. Following one across country was a job that required stamina and determination.

Other vehicles and contraptions were used by infantry for a variety of purposes such as ambulances, escort wagons, ammunition carts, and light gun carriages that required mule power and added to the animal population of the unit. Those mules were the cause of some frustration from time to time among soldiers who took care of them, for the long-eared animals had a reputation for being stubborn and stupid. This reputation was not always deserved, for they could be willing workers when properly handled by a good mule skinner.

There was a story about a stable corporal who visited the corral one Sunday morning to check on the mules, which had been turned out for the weekend. Blackie, one of the mules, was lying on his side, legs stiff, his eyes rolled up with the whites showing, no apparent pulse, and from all appearances had passed on to the next life. The corporal attempted to call the post veterinarian but was unable to get medical help. Some action was necessary so the corporal took matters into his own hands and made an entry in the morning report briefly stating the fact as he saw it and ending the matter as far as he was concerned. The entry read, "Mule Blackie, duty to dead."

2d Infantry Division review, Fort Sam Houston, ca. early 1930s. *Courtesy Fort Sam Houston Archives*

But early Monday morning when the corporal prepared to halter the animals for work, he saw, to his surprise, that Blackie was on his feet eating hay with the other mules. The corporal was now faced with a new problem—what to do about his previous entry in the morning report, which could not be changed without admitting his error of judgment regarding the mule's health. After careful thought, he made an entry in the current day's report that solved the problem. The new entry read, "Mule Blackie, dead to duty." The question of the resurrection of the mule was not important as long as the record was complete.

Ted Harley and I had been together about six months when a historical event took place in the army—the horses and mules of the infantry were replaced with motor vehicles and stable call sounded the last time for the 3d Brigade Headquarters mounted section. Our animals were transferred along with

56

others from Fort Sam that were being reassigned, and on the appointed day the entire bunch was formed in a column of twos, haltered together on a picket rope, and started up the road to Fort Sill, Oklahoma, with a detail of wranglers. Those horses were going to walk four hundred miles or more just to save transportation costs.

An era was passing, and considerable publicity was given to the event and some of the old-timers looked on it as a sentimental occasion. A crowd of spectators lined New Braunfels Avenue, and the division band was drawn up on the parade ground to play for those departing. Post photographer Carl Ekmark was there to film the event, and the local newspapers sent reporters out to cover the story.

I was there, too, because I wanted to see Ted Harley for the last time, and I expected him to make a protest of some kind such as causing a stampede or kicking a wrangler out of the saddle. But he disappointed me and walked quietly along with the others as if he didn't care what happened to him. What hurt the most was that he didn't even look back.

The army was never quite the same after that, for a motor vehicle is only a machine, whereas a horse is flesh and blood and has its own ideas, such as they are. Ted Harley may not have been the best saddle mount in the infantry, but he made life exciting and I missed him when he was gone.

CHAPTER EIGHT

Motorized Infantry

In the 1930s there was little support and less money for a motorized army, and the infantry continued to march at the rate of two and a half miles per hour. The field artillery was still horse-drawn and the cavalry was making charges on horseback armed with sabers.

It was not until late in 1934 that the infantry was furnished with motor vehicles to replace the horses and mules, and the face of the United States military forces began to change. After that the 2d Infantry Division was called a motorized division, which gave a false impression because there were not enough vehicles to haul all the infantry in one move and the foot troops continued to hoof it most of the time. By pooling all trucks available, two or three of the six infantry battalions at Fort Sam Houston could be moved at the same time. Each company now had a truck to carry supplies, instead of the six-mule hitch with the covered wagon that had long been used. The escort wagon, the mule-drawn ambulance, the K-cart, and the Matthews machine gun mount became museum pieces.

Brigade, regimental, and battalion staffs, which had always depended on horses to get about in the field, now traveled in comfort in sedans while the enlisted men of headquarters units rode in station wagons, or carryalls as they were called. Artillery batteries used trucks to tow their guns, with carriages and caissons rolling on rubber tires instead of the iron-rimmed wheels that were standard on the old equipment.

2d Infantry Division at Fort Sam Houston, ca. 1938, shortly after being motorized. *Courtesy Fort Sam Houston Archives*

When the change was made, 3d Brigade Headquarters Company was allotted three trucks of two and a half tons' capacity, four station wagons, and two motorcycles. These vehicles were for the use of the brigade staff and the forty-five enlisted men of headquarters company. The brigade commander continued to use his Buick sedan.

We received the new transport with some misgivings, and there was considerable discussion as to whether motors could do the job as well as animals when in the field. One thing was certain—handling vehicles would be different from taking care of horses and mules. The company had one chauffeur on the roster, a corporal who drove the general's sedan, but he kept the same job so was of no help with the new vehicles. Several men could drive Fords and Chevrolets, but the trucks were bigger, faster, and came with multiple gears, which were new to all of us.

The immediate need was to find men who could drive the machines. Fortunately, there were plenty of volunteers, for every country boy who had looked at the rear end of a mule going down a cotton row was eager to get behind the wheel of a truck. Half the men in the company qualified on this point.

The motorcycles were the three-wheeled type with sidecar, designed to replace the horse-mounted messengers who rode across country with dispatches. This machine was supposed to save the manpower, horsepower, feed, and forage required by the use of animals, as well as saving a great deal of time by traveling faster. The planners who came up with this idea had overlooked history, for the same thing had been tried in World War I and was a failure. That failure was one of the reasons for the continued use of the horse following World War I.

But everybody wanted at least to ride in the sidecar if he couldn't be the driver, and for several weeks the motorcycle was number one on the popularity list. Then we gave it back to the quartermaster. The motorcycle was unsatisfactory in bad weather or for traveling over rough terrain, neither of which bothered a horse if the rider could take the punishment. The motorcycle was again abandoned as a military vehicle, and a few years later the jeep was developed for use in the field. An unfortunate result of the motorcycle tryout was that several men in the outfit bought two-wheelers and were victims of accidents, and one man was killed.

In 1938 the 2d Division units at Fort Sam Houston were fully motorized. The army was moving toward mechanization, although the cavalry was still on horseback and some field artillery regiments were horse-drawn. The pay was still the same, beginning at twenty-one dollars a month, and a truck driver was not considered to be more skilled than a mule skinner.

Training in the use of vehicles for tactical operations occupied much of the time during that first year, and it soon became apparent that the horseless carriage had some advantages over animals. Motors did not have to be fed at six o'clock every morning, they did not require exercise when not in use, nor did they kick or bite their riders. On the other hand, we couldn't take them out for a pleasure ride on Sunday as we had the horses.

An attempt was made to inject some competition and sport into motorization by staging a "road-e-o," a sort of gymkhana with trucks. Changing wheels and driving a test course were two of the events, and vehicles were judged on appearance and maintenance. One of these gymkhanas was tried at Fort Sam Houston in an attempt to work up enthusiasm and develop esprit de corps among chauffeurs and mechanics, but it was a pretty dull exhibition. It couldn't touch a horse show.

During the summer of 1938 all enlisted men of 3d Brigade Headquarters Company were attached to the 23d Infantry for field training to test the division in motorized operations. The 2d Battalion of the regiment needed a sergeant major, and I was assigned the job.

The commanding officer of the 23d was Col. A. W. Lane, an outstanding officer whose service went back to the Boxer Rebellion in China in 1900. In 1941, after he had been promoted to brigadier general, I served on his staff as a first lieutenant at Camp Roberts, California.

Maj. E. A. Kindervater was commanding officer of the 2d Battalion, 23d Infantry. The adjutant was a second lieutenant named James Willis, a recent graduate of the military academy, and supplies were the responsibility of a sergeant named Lucey. Willis was called "mister" by the major, as that had been the custom before World War I when he had entered the army. Major Kindervater referred to Sergeant Lucey as Lieutenant Lucey, but whether this was by intent or mistake was unknown. It embarrassed Lucey to be called "Lieutenant" as much as it did Willis to be called "mister," the service being what it was in those days, but it was amusing to the rest of us.

The high point of this training came when the 2d Division traveled to the Mineral Wells Military Reservation in north Texas. The truck column made a leisurely move of three days

61

from Fort Sam to the maneuver area, camping beside the road each night. Campsites were easy to find because there was plenty of open space along the roads we used.

This exercise included infantry tactical operations, using motor vehicles for troop movements, hauling supplies, and towing heavy weapons. Instead of hiking cross-country in a direct line over the sandy Texas plains, infantry troops crowded into two-and-a-half-ton trucks for long hauls over dirt roads to the destination. At times it took longer to ride than to walk, and the troops sweltered under canvas truck canopies.

After a week on the Mineral Wells Reservation, the 2d Division returned to Fort Sam Houston in a forced motor march, covering the 250 miles in twelve hours, with only brief stops for lunch and to refuel from gasoline tank trucks parked on the side of the road. This was the first motor movement by a large U.S. force over that long a distance to test the mobility of the motorized infantry division. It proved a success, and the days of long foot marches were history.

On this exercise an experiment in field communications was tried on the recommendation of Signal Corps personnel. A signal section with a corporal in charge was attached to the infantry battalion to handle radio and telephone messages; the Signal Corps people believed they could do the job better than infantry soldiers.

The same method had been tried in the past and was not successful, but Signal Corps planners insisted on doing it again. The disadvantage was that men from the Signal Corps were not familiar with the infantry units or tactics, which tended to slow communication instead of speeding it up. After these tests were completed, the Signal Corps withdrew its recommendation and the infantry continued to provide its own field communications.

During the mid-1930s there was no training in tank support for infantry in the 2d Division because only a limited number of light tanks were available to the entire army. In 1931 a small mechanized force consisting of several hundred men equipped with armored cars, tanks, and some artillery was stationed at Fort Eustis, Virginia. This group was organized on an experimental basis and was abandoned in the same year, for lack of money. Various mechanized vehicles were tested by the cavalry units at Fort Knox, Kentucky, in 1933, but it was not until 1938 that an American-designed tank was approved by the War Department for production. The apparent lack of interest in armored vehicles by U.S. government planners at the time when European armies were rapidly developing mechanized forces now seems incredible.

Our first tank units were organized in 1940, when a mechanized cavalry brigade was formed at Fort Knox and an armored infantry regiment was activated at Fort Benning, Georgia. These units were the genesis of the armored divisions that fought in Africa and Europe in World War II.

But it took time to change horsemen into truck drivers, and some never made it. When the 3d Brigade was motorized, several men transferred to the cavalry at border posts so they could have a horse to ride. We had one mule skinner who didn't want anything to do with the new machines. "This army is not for me," he said and next payday drew the few dollars he had coming and went over the hill.

CHAPTER NINE

Single Men in Barracks

It was an army for single men, with a system designed for maximum performance of military duty and a minimum of outside problems. The army did not enlist married men. There was no regulation to prohibit marriage, but an enlisted man was required to obtain permission to marry from his company commander or he could not reenlist at the completion of his term of service. This eliminated a great deal of trouble for the army and saved the United States a lot of money because few professional soldiers would give up military service for a wife.

The pay of the lower ranks was too meager to support a family, and there were no special family benefits to cover the added expenses incurred by dependents. If married, with or without permission, a man could draw his ration allowance in cash, but this was of scant help because he was charged for meals taken in the mess hall when on duty, leaving little extra money to take home.

Noncommissioned officers of the first three grades, the staff, technical, or first, and master sergeants, were governed by different regulations and, if married, were furnished quarters on the post. They made up a small fraction of the enlisted ranks, however. Those senior noncommissioned officers who were bachelors lived in private rooms in barracks and when off duty pursued their own interests, generally keeping aloof from the lower ranks.

But the majority of soldiers who made up the line compa-

Headquarters 9th Infantry mess hall, Fort Sam Houston, in the late 1930s. *Courtesy Fort Sam Houston Archives*

nies, batteries, and troops were single, and they took their fun where they found it, in bars, dance halls, or games of chance, with nice women or women not so nice, as long as their pay lasted. When a man was broke he stayed on the post, went to the movies on credit, played pool in the dayroom, or fired small-caliber weapons on the company's indoor range. Some even read books.

A line of honkytonks stretched for several blocks south of the Fort Sam Houston main gate along North New Braunfels Avenue, and business boomed while soldiers had money. Business slowed the second week of the month when soldiers invariably went broke and could not raise enough cash for a few beers. The price was ten cents a bottle. The last half of the month saw trade reduced to those few men who had been lucky at cards or dice or had been on duty and prevented from celebrating earlier with their comrades. Then payday came again and the cycle was repeated.

There was nothing to set one bar apart from the next, for all served the same brands of beer, mostly Lone Star and Pearl, and the jukeboxes played the same popular country and western tunes. All reeked of stale beer and stale cigarettes, and if the women were different it was in size, shape, and age but not in motive. The consensus among perceptive and sober soldiers was that the women were out to fleece as many men as possible in as short a time as possible.

One of the beauties of North New Braunfels Avenue was a big and aggressive redhead fondly called Division Red, who hung out in one of the more popular bistros and whose announced goal was to lay every soldier of the 2d Division. She didn't succeed; she must have overestimated her own ability as well as overlooked the competition, which was considerable.

For a change in entertainment there was Westside San Antonio. The Longhorn Saloon on Houston Street boasted the longest bar in the world and the largest pair of steer horns anywhere. Around the corner was the Texas Star Taxi Dance Hall, featuring the fastest band west of the Brazos, so quick with a dance number that a dollar string of tickets disappeared in a hostess's bosom quicker than a snake down a gopher hole. The place also sold watered-down whiskey at pumped-up prices.

There were other places known only by street numbers, such as 410 or 629, where the bar was only a front and the real business of the house was transacted in back rooms. It would not be the truth to say that all soldiers visited these places, for some avoided them because they found their fun elsewhere or because of principle. There were even a few who did not recognize the sinful temptations they offered.

We were in a bull session in the dayroom of 3d Brigade Headquarters Company on one occasion when a lad who had just joined the outfit told of his experience on the Westside.

"Last night I went to a movie in town and then had a beer

on Matamoros Street," he related. "On the way to the bus it started to rain and I didn't have my raincoat, but a lady standing in the door of an apartment that I passed asked me to come in. I went inside so I wouldn't get wet and sat in the parlor while she made some coffee. I stayed until it stopped raining and she told me to come back again when I was in the neighborhood. She sure was a nice lady."

There was brief silence before the group broke into wild belly laughs. The place was a well-known "sporting house."

Some soldiers could find trouble wherever they went just as the natural result of being alive. Maybe it was because of boredom, or a sense of toughness that had to be tested, or general devilment, but sooner or later they drank too much liquor, or fought over some imaginary wrong, or had trouble with a woman, or all of these.

One night the military police brought a 3d Brigade Head-quarters soldier back to the company and charged him with fighting a civilian, which was frowned on as poor public relations. Our man had a simple explanation for the encounter.

"I was standing on a corner downtown when a civilian walked up to me and asked for a match. I gave him the match and we started talking."

"What caused the fight?" a buddy asked.

"Well, we talked a while and then we started fighting. That's all there was to it."

It just happened for no reason at all.

But a man didn't have to go to a New Braunfels Avenue bar or the Westside to have a good time.

One weekend Pvt. Bill Maitland, a friend from McAllen, Texas, and I drove there to visit his parents and take his girl and her sister to a dance. I owned a well-worn Chevy coupe, and it took all day of steady driving to cover the three hundred or so miles through flat ranch country.

It was monotonous going, and on the way we amused ourselves by shooting at crows in the road with a pistol I carried in the car, a common practice among cowboys and oil field roughnecks as well as soldiers. Every road sign was punctuated with bullet holes, and the glass insulators on telephone poles had a high casualty rate. It was only another way to let off steam, and there was no harm meant.

After the dance on Saturday night we took the girls home and then went to Bill's house. He didn't go inside but said he wanted to go back and see his girl again and asked if he could take the car. That was all right with me, and I didn't see him until the following morning.

The next day on the way back to Fort Sam, Bill was very quiet, which was unusual for him as he always had something to say. To enliven the trip I got the pistol out and was going to shoot some crows, but the cartridges were all gone. There had been plenty the night before so I asked Bill what had happened to them. He said that when he went back to see his girl again they drove out in the country and he fired all the ammunition just for the hell of it, shooting at mesquite trees, fence posts, or aimlessly out the car window. When he started shooting, his girl got scared and carried on as though she expected to be killed, and he had to calm her down. That was all he would say about it, which was not like him.

When we returned to the barrack, Bill was still not in his normal good-natured mood, and I asked him if he was feeling all right.

He looked sort of foolish and said, "I'm going to marry the girl."

"Oh," I said. "Is that all?"

"Is that all?" he repeated. "I won't be able to reenlist."

It was the end of another brilliant military career.

An alternative to marriage was to "shack up" with a woman, thereby reaping the benefits of wedded bliss without the legal entanglements, but this arrangement was seldom satisfactory. It could be troublesome if the woman cared to protect her common-law rights or showed up at the outfit on payday and demanded part of the soldier's pay from the company commander.

For every hundred men there must have been a hundred different reasons for joining the army, but for some it didn't make any sense.

One of those who seemed to lack most, if not all, of the requirements was a man named Montgomery, a normal young fellow who was never in trouble but who certainly wasn't cut out to be a soldier.

After completing his recruit training in a line outfit, he was assigned to division headquarters as a clerk, which suited him as well as anything could, but all he really wanted to do was play the pipe organ. He would practice on the chapel organ every chance he got and all he talked about around the barrack was music, which was a disadvantage for the rest of us as we didn't know anything about the subject. I guess we listened out of ignorance.

One evening Montgomery ran into the barrack and announced that the chaplain was going to let him play for the Sunday services and this was his chance to show what he could do best. It was a big day for him. He was even going to wear a black choir robe for the performance.

Early Sunday morning Montgomery got dressed in the robe and paraded up and down the squad room asking everybody if he looked all right. We looked him over and said he looked great, but there was one smart aleck in the bunch who said the first sergeant would have to make a final inspection and give his approval. The joker said this with a straight face and in such a serious tone of voice that Montgomery didn't see any humor in it, but he didn't know the topkick as well as the rest of us did. The first sergeant was called Bull and for good reason. He was a big, burly fellow, who didn't tolerate any nonsense from recruits.

As several of us watched from a safe distance, Montgomery breezed into the orderly room and asked Bull if his robe looked all right. Instead of exploding, Bull looked Montgomery over carefully, had him turn around so he could see the back of the robe, and said, "It looks just fine, but it needs to be pulled up in front a little." When Montgomery made the adjustment, Bull said, "Now, that's better, but you can't walk to the chapel in the robe, you might get it dirty. I'll call the motor pool for a car to drive you over."

That response deflated us considerably because we had expected the topkick to give Montgomery a chewing for bothering him, but the best was yet to come.

We went out on the barrack porch to see how Montgomery handled the robe when he got into the car, thinking we might get a laugh.

There was a laugh, all right, but it was on us. It was the general's car that came to pick Montgomery up, and the driver, a corporal, got out and opened the door for that buck private, then drove off with him in the backseat where the general usually sat. None of us ever said anything more about the robe inspection and neither did Montgomery. He didn't know there was anything unusual about it.

On payday at 3d Brigade Headquarters Company, after the company commander left to go to his quarters, the poker players gathered in the dayroom. If it was on a weekday the game would last until reveille the following day, and if payday was on Saturday it might run nonstop until Monday.

We played straight poker by strict rules. Wild games were limited to seven-card stud, with an occasional deuces wild hand to keep everyone awake. There was no jawbone, or credit, only cash, table stakes. If a player went broke he could borrow from a nonplayer but not from anyone in the game. We didn't play against our own money. There was no liquor because the noncommissioned officer in charge of quarters forbade it to protect his stripes, and his authority was respected even though he might be junior to some of the players. Rank carried a lot of weight among regulars even when off duty.

Noncommissioned officers were not supposed to play in a game with privates, but it was done. We all knew each other too well to draw that fine a line.

There was no break in the game for meals, but a buddy

would go to a restaurant on New Braunfels Avenue for sandwiches and coffee from time to time.

There might be two hundred or three hundred dollars in the game, sometimes more—a considerable amount of cash for Depression days. If a soldier could win fifty bucks he was on top of the world.

Dice was a popular game, too, and there would usually be a crowd shooting crap on the pool table at the same time the card game was in session. One difference was that the crap shooters traveled from game to game, moving to various outfits as the winners challenged each other for the big pots. Poker players more often stayed in the same game month after month.

When John Travers was first sergeant of 3d Brigade Headquarters Company he kept a thousand dollars in cash in the company safe, money he had saved during his service in China. This caused me some concern because I was company clerk and carried a key to the safe.

One day I mentioned my worry to John, and he said, "Forget it," which was a compliment I did not forget. Then he said, "There is one thing I want you to remember. Unless I am sober, don't let me take any money out of that safe.'

For several months the roll of bills remained untouched by the "top," lying in the little iron box with the secret code books and cryptographic devices and some papers called the "tan plan." The tan plan contained orders for the defense against any enemy who might attack Texas through Mexico. That aroused my curiosity, and I tried to find out who would go to all that trouble, but no one I talked to had any idea. Anyone familiar with northern Mexico would stay out of the place. Gen. John Pershing learned that lesson when he chased Pancho Villa across the border in 1915 and Villa lost him in the mountains.

One payday, after Travers and a couple of other experts had cleaned out everybody in the company crap game, two sports from the 9th Infantry drifted in. They had busted a big game in their outfit and wanted some new action. They were pretty good with the galloping dominoes and in a couple of hours had most of the money in the game, including a hundred or so from Sergeant Travers. This was money from his pay and winnings and not from his roll in the safe.

When Travers and the two shooters from the 9th were the only players left in the game, it began to get serious. Bets were raised and everyone who hadn't headed for the honkytonks crowded around the pool table, which was the scene of action. We were all hoping that the top would clean the visiting dudes, not only out of loyalty to the outfit but because it would be a lot easier to get along with John if he came out the winner.

But the competition was rough, and pretty soon John was down to his last sawbuck. He called me over and said he wanted a couple of hundred out of the safe. "I can take these guys," he said. "They've just had a run of good luck."

I got the two hundred for him, but it didn't last long and John wanted another two hundred. His luck was still bad, and that money disappeared, too. We watched the visitors to see if there was any funny business, but everything seemed to be on the level.

John wanted more money, and when I cautioned him to take it easy with his bankroll he said, "Get the rest of it. My luck is bound to change. I remember what I told you and I'm as sober as the chaplain."

The top knew what he was doing, for he won back his money and had a couple of hundred of the visitors' cash when they quit the game. John gave me the thousand to put back in the safe, keeping his pay and winnings for recreational purposes.

"How did you do it?" I asked him. "It looked like you were going broke, but you finished a winner."

"Patience," the topkick said. "I learned that in China. The Chinese say if you wait long enough your luck will change. They have more patience than any people in the world, and I guess some of it rubbed off on me."

The boredom of barracks life produced considerable horse-play, on duty as well as off, as soldiers found ways to burn off excess energy and have fun.

All the old tricks—shortsheeting, the hotfoot, shoes tied together, knotted socks—were repeated at every opportunity. Each new recruit who joined the outfit was sent to the supply room for such nonexistent equipment as left-handed ramrods and bunk stretchers, only to draw the wrath of an annoyed supply sergeant.

Ingenious schemes were invented, some of which were marvels of imagination, to play a joke on a buddy or try a prank that fell just short of breaking regulations or causing serious trouble. Most soldiers knew how far they could go without a breach of orders or trespassing on forbidden ground prohibited by the "customs of the service."

One such joke was originated by two headquarters clerks who wrote a fake order that appeared to be official in every detail. It ordered the discharge of an unsuspecting friend under a regulation that probably had never been used before. Puzzled, the soldier took the order to the company clerk to find out why he was being kicked out of his happy home and learned that the regulation covered the discharge of an enlisted man for "extreme ugliness."

Sometimes a scheme would have a selfish motive. One man in our outfit sent himself a telegram with a spurious offer of a tryout with a professional baseball team. He wanted a pass to evade weekend duty, but the trick did not deceive the first sergeant. The soldier was the poorest athlete in the company.

Occasionally a prank would get an entire regiment in an uproar. At reveille each morning the 23d Infantry guard fired a 75-mm gun loaded with a blank round to make sure everybody would rise and shine. The guard was supposed to check the bore before loading but frequently that chore was overlooked, and one Sunday morning when the gun was fired a rock sailed across the parade ground and crashed in a barrack. The outfit turned out on the double. There was an investigation, but the prankster who loaded the boulder into the cannon was never identified. It was rumored that the perpetrator was known, but his name was not revealed to the investigating officer, for the men stuck together.

The soldier suspected of the deed was on his way to the barracks from a Saturday night spree when he passed the gun, which gave him the idea. He wrapped a rock in newspaper and rammed it down the barrel. The paper acted as wadding, allowing the gas expansion from the blank round to propel the stone a hundred yards or more across the parade into the company barrack.

Thereafter, on orders of the regimental commander, the guard was careful to inspect the bore before firing.

Kipling was right about single men in barracks: they don't grow into plaster saints, for youth demands action and the barrack is not a monastery, but a man could find friends there, and to many regulars it was the only home they knew.

CHAPTER TEN

Foreign Service

When a soldier got fed up with stateside duty or got the wanderlust, he could pull a hitch in foreign service, and there were men who made a career of traveling between the States and overseas stations. The choices were relatively few when compared with the worldwide activities of today's United States Army, but they covered a wide range of climate and territory.

There were garrisons in Panama, the Philippines, Puerto Rico, China, Alaska, and Hawaii, most of them infantry regiments but with a sprinkling of support troops and army air corps units. Some posts in Texas were considered the same as foreign service because of terrain and language, but although there may have been certain resemblances, the official viewpoint did not see it that way.

The desirability of a foreign station was rumored to increase with distance, and the 15th Infantry in Tientsin, China, was said to be as close to paradise as a soldier would ever get. Many men who became dissatisfied in the States enlisted for that regiment.

Barrack gossip had it that Chinese peasants were hired to do kitchen police and fatigue duty and to serve as orderlies for all ranks, including privates. A soldier didn't have to clean his rifle, shine his shoes, or polish his brass; all such menial jobs were done for him by hired Chinese. An enlisted man was required only to pull guard duty, stand parade for visiting diplomats, and draw his pay. Even reveille report each morning was made by the head houseboy while the troops slumbered.

A first sergeant out of the 15th was assigned to 3d Brigade Headquarters Company in a swap for one of our sergeants, and we awaited with interest the arrival of the new topkick. We were curious, not apprehensive, for the job had to be filled by someone and we had nothing to say about it anyway.

The new sergeant was John Travers, a short, broad-shouldered, deep-chested man who carried a swagger stick, an item of equipment long out of favor stateside, although it was still common in foreign armies and our China forces. It had something to do with being a symbol of authority and showed the Chinese who was boss. Even more remarkable, John brought with him the bankroll of a thousand dollars, the savings of a dozen years in Tientsin.

As he was a bachelor, the new top moved into a private room in the barrack reserved for the senior noncommissioned officer, something new in our outfit because the previous first sergeant was married. This caused some muttering among the privates, because most of the men did not relish spending twenty-four hours each day under the critical eye of the topkick.

It turned out that there was nothing to worry about. Travers had a friendly manner, while at the same time being firm and dignified. He was an experienced leader who knew his job well and got along with the men of the company, on or off duty.

John confirmed most of the stories about service in China, but one was completely false—enlisted men didn't get to stay in their blankets after first call but had to turn out for reveille just as they did stateside. The biggest advantage was economic. A man's pay went further in Tientsin.

After a year in the States John began to talk about the good times he had on foreign service and the beauty of the tropics.

"Too cold in this country," he complained one day. "My

arthritis is getting worse. Write out a request for transfer to Panama for me and maybe we can work a swap."

There was a first sergeant in Panama who was ready to come stateside, and when the transfer was approved, John went back to foreign service. He took the thousand in cash with him, rolled up in the rubber band, his reserve against the need for financial reinforcements.

Brigade Sgt. Maj. Ed Ward was another outstanding soldier who was a veteran of foreign service. He was a football player and had played on championship teams in Hawaii and in the States. As a recruit he had had an unusual assignment on his first enlistment. Eddie was a big kid and at the age of sixteen told a recruiting sergeant that he was eighteen and enlisted for the 27th Infantry. The recruiting sergeant was also guilty of concealing the facts—he did not tell Eddie the 27th was in Siberia, where the regiment had been sent during World War I. This was not a well-publicized bit of information, and Eddie had never heard of it. He was more than surprised when he was shipped out to Vladivostok.

"When I finished recruit training," Ed recalled, "I was assigned to duty as a guard on a train that ran from Vladivostok to Novosibirsk and for six months I rode that train across Siberia, back and forth, twenty-four hundred miles each way. The supply sergeant would give me enough grub for the trip and I was on my own."

"What were you guarding?" I queried.

"I never found out," Ed said. "No one took the trouble to tell me."

"Did you have any trouble?" I asked. There were spy stories in those days, too.

"Never heard a shot fired," Ed said. "The Russians were fighting among themselves, but that was farther west. The worst part was the monotony of riding through the desolate country."

Foreign service privates were a different breed. They had restless feet and a faraway look in their eyes and when dissatisfied with a unit they would request a transfer and move on. These men seldom served out an enlistment in the States and were not concerned about being reduced in rank to get a transfer. If they were stateside when their enlistment expired, they would usually go to the nearest port and enlist for the foreign garrison they fancied at the time. They would come and go, do their duty well, seldom cause any trouble, and were generally good soldiers, but they never seemed to find the outfit that suited them.

"There were only two good outfits in the army," one veteran private confided to me when he applied for a transfer to Hawaii. "The one I just left and the one I'm going to."

It took me a while to figure that out.

There was a reverse side to the foreign service, too, for most regiments had a few Puerto Ricans, Filipinos, and Europeans who made a career of the United States Army. A Puerto Rican who had served in the 65th Infantry on the island or a Filipino who had been a scout could reenlist for stateside duty.

Carlos Garcia, the bugler for Company D, 9th Infantry, was a former Philippine Scout. He was a cheerful, good-natured man who got along well with other soldiers.

His outfit was camped next to mine on a field exercise on one occasion and we were swapping stories about our homes and service.

"Why did you leave your country and come to the States?" I asked him.

"The money," he said. "The pay of the regular army is twice that of the scouts."

The base pay of a private first class was then thirty dollars a month.

The army was a sort of foreign legion and in the 3d Brigade we had German, English, Italian, and French boys as well as Puerto Ricans and Filipinos. If they landed in the States and couldn't find a job, they would join the army if they could pass the IQ test and physical examination. Citizenship was not required, although most of them became citizens after staying

Philippine Scouts in the U.S. Army, ca. 1930s. *Courtesy National Archives*

in the service an enlistment or two.

We even had a Lithuanian, John Kulikofsky. John preferred the foreign service, but for a change of scenery he would put in an enlistment stateside now and then. He was an all-around good soldier who could be anything in the infantry—rifleman, automatic weapons man, radio man, line man. He was a good athlete as well.

When Kulikofsky and I were attached to the 23d Infantry, there was a sergeant named Gordon in the outfit who constantly heckled John. It was done in a friendly way, but the sergeant never let up.

"How do you pronounce your name?" Gordon would ask John, although he knew very well, and when John would tell him, Gordon would keep up his razzing tactics. "What kind of a name is that?" Gordon would ask. When John would say it was Lithuanian, which he did dozens of times, the sergeant would say, "If I had a name like that I would change it."

This heckling went on all one summer, and John took it good-naturedly.

Then one day when the sergeant was riding him pretty hard, John said, "I'm going to take your advice and change my name. Do you want to know what it is going to be?"

"Tell me," said the sergeant.

"Gordon," John said. Later he applied for a change of name, which was approved. The sergeant never mentioned the subject again, but we didn't let him forget there was a Lithuanian named Gordon in the outfit.

CHAPTER ELEVEN

Pay Call

One formation that all soldiers were sure to make was pay call, the day the eagle flew.

On the last workday of the month, the Old Man would go to the post finance office and draw the outfit's pay in cash. He would be back by recall, just before noon, and the first sergeant would have the men lined up for the most important event on the schedule.

If the last day of the month fell on Sunday, payday was the day before. Even if a man drew his money on Saturday and then went over the hill or to the guardhouse, the army wouldn't lose for it couldn't get anything out of a soldier the next day anyway.

The outfit would form up outside the orderly room, where the commanding officer was sitting at a table with stacks of currency and piles of coins in front of him ready to count out. Pay was in cash, mostly new bills that had a bright, rich look, and the change was figured out to the penny by the finance officer so it would all come out even with everyone getting the exact amount due.

When the Old Man was ready, the first sergeant would call each man's name, alphabetically by rank, and the soldier would march briskly up to the pay table, come to attention, and salute smartly, giving his name, rank, and serial number in one breath. The commanding officer would return the salute, and the first sergeant would then read the amount due the soldier from the payroll. The officer would count out the cash and hand it to the soldier, who would salute again, about-face, and head for the door.

The temporarily rich soldier normally had one of three goals on his mind at the moment—sprint for the nearest game of chance, take off for his favorite bar on New Braunfels Avenue, or grab the next bus to San Antonio's Westside for a visit to his favorite pleasure palace. If the outfit was in the field, payday was held on schedule, without regard for location or weather, and as soon as the Old Man disappeared, the games of chance started. Nor was it unusual, if in the field, for the soldier to head across the prairie to the nearest town with a cantina and then try to find the outfit before morning.

With the meager pay a soldier received before World War II the money didn't last long. Starting with the base pay for a private at $21 per month it rose to $30 for a private first class. A corporal drew a base of $42, and a sergeant, sometimes a veteran of twenty or twenty-five years service with a war or two behind him, drew a base salary of $54 per month. The upper noncommissioned grades fared better, a staff sergeant drawing $72, first and technical sergeants $84, and a master sergeant the sum of $126 as their base pay. Because most men, especially the noncoms, had more than four years' service, they drew longevity pay on top of the base. This additional pay, or "fogy," increased base pay by 5 percent for each four years' good time.

Privates and privates first class could also draw extra pay as specialists in a variety of fields, for example, as bugler, teamster, cook, radio operator, etc. Pay for specialist first class was thirty dollars per month; second class, twenty-five dollars; third class, twenty dollars; fourth class, fifteen dollars; fifth class, six dollars; and sixth class, three dollars. Specialist pay was not increased by a fogy.

If an enlisted man was placed on special duty away from his unit and was not furnished rations and quarters he was paid an allowance to cover this expense, amounts which were determined at the time.

But it did not add up very fast, and after deductions were made there wasn't much left. Deductions were for expenses that all soldiers had such as barber bills, tailor bills, tobacco, toilet articles, tickets to the post movie theater, and similar items. Ten cents a month went to the Old Soldiers Home at Washington, D.C., and for that princely sum a retired soldier was entitled to spend the rest of his days there. These bills were charged against a man's pay on a charge sheet by the unit clerk to be deducted from the payroll, and in effect were an advance on the man's pay and he never saw the money.

But what he had left was enjoyed to the the fullest, and life was sweet while the money lasted. With beer at ten cents a bottle, cheap whiskey, and a movie downtown at thirty-five cents, a couple of dollars could give a man a night on the town, and if he couldn't make it back to the post he could stay at the YMCA for half a buck.

The gamblers stayed with the cards or dice until they were broke or until they broke the game or until reveille stopped the fun. A few were lucky, and some were consistent winners who picked their games and played close to the vest. Then there were men who somehow always had a bankroll to back them in a new game, lend a buck or two to a buddy, or go out on the town the week before payday.

When a man's pay was gone and he felt the need for cash, there were ways to raise money, all of them illegal or imprudent. It was a common practice for a man to draw movie tickets and post exchange coupons on his account and then sell them to local saloonkeepers. The coupons would go at half price, and the soldier would spend the money in the same bar, paying full price for beer and whiskey. The saloonkeeper would sell the coupons to other soldiers at less than face value but at more than he paid the original owner, thus making two profits. This practice violated regulations but was overlooked by commanding officers, and no one ever got into trouble over such a transaction.

The loan business was also common. In every regiment there were men who would lend money to their buddies who had a reputation for repaying promptly. The standard loan was four dollars to get five back the next payday. The fact that his figured out to 300 percent simple interest (per annum) didn't stop a soldier from borrowing if he wanted the money badly enough. This form of larceny was prohibited by regulations, but the borrower wanted to protect his source of ready funds and as a result never reported the man who made the loan. Also, incredible as it seems, no one considered the interest rate excessive.

Men coming back to the States from the 15th Infantry in Tientsin were fond of telling how easy it was to clean up on the exchange of dollars for Chinese currency. There were stories of quick profits made in this black-market trading, and many soldiers transferring to the Far East had visions of getting rich by such financial dealings. There was some truth to it, and the same thing took place in Europe following World War II, when there was considerable trading in francs for dollars.

In spite of the low pay, there were men who managed to save money and some who even sent a few dollars home to needy parents. Very rarely did a soldier get money from home, but there was one man in 3d Brigade Headquarters Company who received a share of oil royalties from property owned by his family. This man always had money to spend, but he didn't throw it away. He was a poker player and with his oil-backed bankroll could ride out a streak of bad luck.

For the most part, regulars were satisfied with the pay they received, very likely because all were volunteers who had known what the prospects would be when they enlisted. They made out with what they had, and if a man became dissatisfied he did not reenlist.

But most remained, reenlisting time after time, which was one reason the pay remained low, for it was love of the army and not the pay that kept them on, and the government knew it.

Nor could officers expect to become wealthy in the military service. The pay of the chief of staff, the top man in the army, was $666.67 per month, plus $117.30 for quarters and rations. Major generals received the same pay and allowances as the chief of staff, which seems hardly fair for the chief. Brigadier generals were paid $500 per month, with the same allowances as the other general ranks. Colonels with twenty-six years service drew $466.67, but were paid $500 after thirty years. Lieutenant colonels with twenty years were paid $379.17 per month, and it went to $479.17 after thirty years. Majors with 14 years behind them drew $250, and their top salary was $437.50 at thirty years. Captains with less than 17 years were paid $220 per month, but it could go as high as $375 if they lasted thirty years in that rank. A first lieutenant was worth $166.67 to start, but his pay could go as high as $300 in thirty years, if he hadn't quit before that time. A second lieutenant started at $125 per month, one dollar less than a master sergeant.

The ration allowance was $15.30 per month for all ranks, without dependents.

As with the enlisted men, it apparently was not the pay that kept officers in the army.

CHAPTER TWELVE

Sporting Types

To say that World War II was won on the playing fields of army posts would be an exaggeration, but sports were an important part of military life during the 1930s. Physical contests gave men a chance to work off steam, helped build esprit de corps in regiments, and provided free entertainment for the garrison. This was a fringe benefit enjoyed by all ranks because there was never an admission charge for any sporting event.

The quality of athletics was high, for competition was keen and there were plenty of candidates for both team and individual contests. Athletes who made the regimental teams may not have been professionals in the strict meaning of the word, but they came close. They were allowed all the time necessary to practice, were well coached, and were relieved of duty that would interfere with the sport. There was some recruiting of good athletes, but many volunteered solely to be able to take part in organized athletics. In the Depression years opportunities in professional sports were limited and the pay was low. The security provided by military service was an added benefit.

More soldiers played the game of baseball than any other team sport, for each company put a team on the field and men were encouraged to play. During the summer when troops were in garrison there would be games each afternoon, and off-duty personnel would turn out to cheer their buddies.

There were battalion and regimental leagues, as well as the

interpost leagues, which were the "major leagues" of service baseball. These were made up of outstanding players selected from the company teams for their ability; it was, in effect, a farm system. Managers were officers who had played the game at West Point or other colleges or were senior noncommissioned officers, some with professional experience.

Although a member of a regimental team was a soldier first, he was excused from such unpleasant work details as kitchen police, stable call, or pulling targets during the playing season or when in training. This was an incentive to be on the team, and a man who made the regimental squad could depend on promotion in rank as well. Also, a good baseball player could stay in training and play the game while awaiting a tryout with a minor league team, and more than one man got his chance that way.

The best example was Dizzy Dean, who began his baseball career at Fort Sam Houston in 1928 pitching for the post laundry team. In 1929 Dizzy bought his discharge to play for the San Antonio Public Service Club and the following year began his professional career with a St. Louis Cardinal minor league team. In 1934 he was voted the outstanding athlete of the year by the Associated Press while playing for the Cardinals. For years fans at Fort Sam Houston talked about the way Dizzy could throw a baseball and how Sgt. Jimmy Brought, the coach of the 12th Field Artillery team, saw his potential and helped him get a start.

Boxing was another popular sport. There were few regulars who did not think they could hold their own against all comers, bare-knuckled or with the gloves, and each company would hold impromptu bouts to give every man a chance to put up his dukes. As in other sports, each regiment was represented by a boxing team that took part in an annual tournament at Fort Sam Houston to determine the champion in each weight class. Officially this tournament was for amateurs, but many of the contenders carried professional cards and appeared on fight programs in San Antonio and other cities. A soldier who was good at the manly art could pick up a purse now and then in professional bouts without hurting his amateur status in the army. These fights were battles between boys happy to maul each other in the ring for a purse of ten or twenty dollars. A main event might go as high as a hundred.

One of these bouts took place in San Antonio between a local boxer named Martinez, who was popular with the Mexican American fans, and the Fort Sam welterweight champ, a soldier named Etheridge. The match was held on the west side of town in a small hall that was typical of the old fight clubs—a low-ceilinged, dusty gymnasium that reeked of cigar smoke, stale beer, and sweat. Weekly boxing and wrestling bouts were held in the place, and frequently the fights outside the ring between spectators were better than the brawl on the program.

The match between Martinez and Etheridge received considerable publicity, and the hall was jammed with civilians and soldiers, the crowd being about equally divided. Because the bout had racial overtones as well as pitting civilian against soldier, the San Antonio police department was well represented, on the request of the promoter.

The fight was a battle from start to finish. Both men gave their best, slugging each other from bell to bell until the end of the final round. In the excitement of the contest, the crowd also got worked up, each side cheering its man, with challenges being hurled by the fans, mostly out of bravado. The presence of the police prevented any fisticuffs outside the ring; also, the fight was such a good match that no one wanted to miss any part of it.

By the end of the tenth round the crowd was in such an uproar that the promoter and judges knew there would be trouble if the decision did not suit one of the parties. Since the bout had been close all the way, the ring officials voted the only decision that made sense—they called the fight a draw. Tension eased, everyone was satisfied, and the crowd went home without rioting.

In the late 1930s a trooper named Lew Jenkins, from one of the regiments of the 1st Cavalry Brigade on the border, began to make a name for himself as a lightweight boxer. After winning a string of bouts in army tournaments he started boxing professionally. In 1939 he went to New York, where he broke into the big time and after a number of fights took on Lou Ambers for the world title. Jenkins won the bout by a knockout and held the title for more than year and a half before losing it to Sammy Angott by a decision. Trooper Lew Jenkins had made it to the top, and his buddies in the army were proud of him.

But the sport that drew the biggest crowds was football, and when the 9th Infantry eleven played at Fort Sam Houston there was standing room only in the stadium. The fans could depend on a great performance, not only on the field but by the 9th Infantry band as well, which had almost as many fans as the team.

That band could play rousing, foot-stomping, exciting music, both popular and military, and the crowd showed its appreciation by cheering the musicians as loudly as the athletes. Its trademark tune was "Milenberg Joys." At halftime intermission, the musicians remained seated and played until almost time for the second half of the game to begin. The crowd knew what was coming next, and when the band played the opening bars of "Milenberg Joys" a roar of applause went up. Then the audience became quiet in anticipation. The solo trumpeter stood up in the center of the band, and the crowd gave one more cheer before he played a note. Another hush fell over the stadium.

That trumpeter could work magic with his valve horn, and the chorus of the "Joys" was made to order for him. The clean, clear notes rang out over the stadium, and for a few moments the thousands who listened were hypnotized. When the solo part ended and the trumpeter sat down, the soldiers would go crazy, giving a great cheer and yelling, whistling, and stomping to show their approval. But there was never an encore, no repeat of the performance at the same game. The song would be played at the next game; the soldiers knew this and were satisfied.

Army teams played a pretty fair brand of football, with players coming from the academy at West Point and colleges around the country, as well as the brawny recruits who entered the service from coal mines, sawmills, and ranches.

In the 1930s the 9th Infantry team included several star players who gave the regiment a winning club, one that had an edge on most other army teams. Lt. John Murrell, an All-American from West Point, coached the team, and he had plenty of talent to work with. One player who gave a touch of class to the club was Pvt. Joe Moerschbacher.

Joe had played football at Villanova College and joined the army while passing through Texas looking for a job. He was a fine left-handed passer who was also good at carrying the pigskin, but he was at his best as a kicker. In one game he punted the ball ninety yards. Moerschbacher could be depended on to turn in an outstanding performance, and his buddies always backed him up with some wagering on the game to add to the excitement. No soldier would turn down a chance to win a buck, especially with the odds in his favor.

There was considerable rivalry between the 9th Infantry and 15th Field Artillery, and when their football teams met in the fall of 1937 a group from infantry brigade headquarters planned a financial massacre of the gunners. The infantry team had not lost a game and the artillery club was only fair. With Moerschbacher in the game it looked like a sure chance to make some easy money.

Our bunch of sports pooled all the cash we could raise and came up with a hundred in long green, which at current army pay would be at least a couple of thousand. I was elected to represent the infantry in the transaction.

There was a corporal named Baker in the 15th Field Artillery who kept abreast of such matters, and I looked him up to see if he was interested in covering the investment.

"How many points are you giving?" the gunner asked.

"No points," I said. "The teams are even."

"Nothing doing," said Baker. "The gravel agitators haven't lost a game this season."

I offered to give him a couple of touchdowns, but the artilleryman wouldn't be taken in and we couldn't agree on a wager.

My buddies in brigade headquarters were not happy at losing a chance to double their money, but we went to the game just the same to see Joe Moerschbacher boot the pigskin and hear the trumpeter play "Milenberg Joys."

To the surprise of the garrison, Moerschbacher was bottled up the entire game, the underdogs played like champions, and the artillery team won by four touchdowns. The loss by the infantry was a disappointment, but our investment club went home in a happy mood—we still had our hundred dollars.

On the way back to the barracks we stopped at the canteen for coffee, and there was my friend the artillery corporal having the same. It was sad to see a strong man put his head on the table and cry like a babe when we razzed him for not taking our bet.

The sports program did a great deal more than provide competition and entertainment for the peacetime army. It trained men to be leaders on the athletic field and later, when it counted most, many of those men were leaders on the battlefield.

CHAPTER THIRTEEN

Buck Fever

When fall came to the Hill Country of Texas and garrison duty settled down to routine, we took to the field after white-tailed deer, which were plentiful in that part of the state. Our familiar training ground, the Leon Springs Reservation, was open to military personnel for hunting, and many ranchers would permit hunters on their land, sometimes charging a small fee. Times were hard, and a buck, greenbacked or four-footed, was worth something.

The white-tail was new game for me, for there had been no open season on deer in my home state of Missouri for many years, but there were plenty of experts to tell a beginner how to go about it.

"The only time you will see deer is early morning or late evening, " one hunter said. "They take cover and sleep in the middle of the day."

"When the weather is warm you might as well stay at home," another advised. "A deer will find cool shade and hide on a warm day."

"The only way to hunt is to take a stand and let the animal come to you," a third explained. "You'll never walk up on a Texas white-tail. They are too wary."

There were four of us in that first hunting party: Joe Collins, Louis Loucks, George Odell, and me, all of Headquarters Company, 3d Brigade. We drove out to Leon Springs in the middle of the night in Louis's new Chevy, which he had just bought with his World War I bonus money, and waited for dawn to break. There was a chill in the air and no wind, a good omen.

Odell had his star-gauged Springfield along, the one he had bought at the ordnance depot in San Antonio and used when firing for record. He was proud of that piece and never failed to qualify as an expert rifleman.

"Men," George said, patting the Springfield, "if there is a deer on the reservation, we'll have meat on the table. This baby can bring one down as far as I can see."

None of us had been hunting with George, but we had seen him shoot, and there was no argument.

When it was light enough to see to avoid the cactus, we spread out in the oak scrub and took stands a quarter-mile or more apart. Dawn came slowly, and what appeared to be feeding deer took shape among the trees. I sighted in on each of them, my heart beating rapid-fire, then held the trigger as the targets became boulders and clumps of mesquite in the rising sun. Then, after a long wait, there was a loud snort from a nearby ravine and a buck with a huge rack of antlers bounded over the crest of a ridge half a mile away. The animal was moving too fast and the range was too great to risk a shot, and I settled back for another wait.

For an hour or more I remained on my stand without seeing another deer, then moved to a spot where there was better observation but saw no game at the new location. Since no shots came from the direction taken by the other hunters, it appeared that they were having no better luck.

The morning passed as I moved from stand to stand, through country that showed abundant sign of deer that had recently fed and rested in the area. The terrain was familiar because the brigade had maneuvered through it many times, and I was on home ground. After eating the cheese sandwich and orange I had brought from the mess hall, I gave up hope of bagging a deer from a stand and, in violation of the advice I had received, shouldered my Winchester as if walking post and sauntered toward the top of a nearby hill for a better view. It was now midday, the sun had chased away the morning chill, and another of the rules was broken, for it was as hot as the hobs of hell and a sensible deer should have been asleep somewhere in cool shade.

Blundering along with my rifle at a careless shoulder-arms, I crashed through a thick stand of live oak and came head-on with a large buck that was browsing in a grassy glade. There was a moment of uncertainty brought on by the surprise meeting before I fixed my sights on an exposed shoulder of the animal and squeezed the trigger. The buck went down, and the hard work of dressing out the meat began.

The sound of my shot brought Joe Collins to give me a hand, and we carried the carcass out to the trail, where it could easily be loaded on the car. As we reached the trail, a shot came from the direction in which we had last seen Odell.

"George got one," Joe said, confident that Odell would not miss. "Let's go back and help him."

The single report indicated a hit, so I agreed, but while Joe was speaking, two more shots came from the same spot and, in seconds, two more reports followed in rapid-fire cadence. Joe and I hurried toward the sound, wondering what had happened.

A half-mile up the valley Odell was sitting on the ground, rifle across his knees, bolt open. He appeared dazed.

"I missed him," George mumbled. "There was a big buck right in front of me at fifty yards and I missed five times. I don't know what happened.

"Buck fever," Joe explained. "That is all it was. Sooner or later it happens to every deer hunter."

It was incredible but true. In his excitement, George had missed five shots at point-blank range at a target a schoolboy could have hit with a rock.

But that was not the last of Odell's bad luck on the trip, for as we left the reservation the military police at the checkpoint impounded his Springfield for the remainder of deer season before returning it to him. Although the rifle belonged to George, enlisted men were not authorized to use military weapons for hunting. He had to wait until another time to cure his buck fever.

We took the deer I bagged back to San Antonio and had a fiesta. The whole outfit was invited to the party. Louis Loucks's wife Maria was an expert at making tacos, and deer tacos covered with spicy Mexican sauce and washed down with Lone Star are hard to beat.

There was good hunting in Real County in south-central Texas, and one season six of us spent a week on the John Mears ranch, a spread of several thousand acres along the Frio River. It was wild, rough terrain, but feed, water, and cover were plentiful and game was abundant. In the party were three noncoms from the artillery brigade—Harmonson, McCartney, and Young—and Joe Collins, Harry Hollon, and me from the infantry brigade. We moved into a line cabin used by the ranch hands when working in the area and went after deer.

As a start Mears showed us a different method of hunting that he had developed, which may have been slightly illegal and certainly was frowned on by some sportsmen. But it was original and sometimes effective so it wasn't all bad if you were trying to put meat on the table. Rancher Mears used a tame deer as a decoy to lead wild bucks to the hunters.

The year before he had found a buck fawn, took it home, and raised it on a bottle. The animal soon became a pet, had the run of the place, and would follow John everywhere he went. When the fawn got older it could easily jump any fence and would roam the country for miles but would always come back to the house. John hung a small bell around the buck's neck so it wouldn't be mistaken for a wild deer and end up on a nearby rancher's table, for some of the local citizens weren't too particular about the game laws and had venison the year round.

John would take the tame buck out in the hills until he found fresh deer sign, then turn it loose while the hunters took stands where there was good observation and got ready for action. The tame buck would run off in the brush following sign until he found a wild buck and then, after a friendly romp, would start home with the wild deer after him. When John's deer ran past the hunters, they could hear the bell and were supposed to hold their fire until the wild one came in range.

It didn't seem fair to play the game that way, but the end result was what counted. Besides, if hunters could run deer on horseback or with dogs, it couldn't be any worse to decoy them with a tame buck. There were a lot of arguments to support the method; still I didn't like the idea and gave it up after the first day. We didn't have any luck with it because John's deer ran off after the wild ones instead of the other way around.

I had better success by taking a stand along a game trail and waiting for a buck to show up. In that way I bagged two deer during the hunt. One of these was a good-sized buck that field-dressed over a hundred pounds. It was at least a mile back to the cabin, and I was faced with the task of packing the meat down a mountainside and through a canyon, over rough terrain all the way.

After dressing out the carcass, I carried it a hundred yards over the trail, with the load getting heavier at each step. I had seen pictures of hunters with a deer over their shoulders, striding through the forest, and it looked easy, but it didn't work that way for me. When I got the animal on my shoulders, the head and feet would drag on the ground or become tangled in the brush, making walking difficult. Also, the rifle was awkward to handle with the load on my back, adding to the problem. After considering all possibilities, including dumping the meat in the canyon and forgetting the entire thing, I decided to go for help.

There were coyotes in the neighborhood on the prowl for a free meal so I hung the meat in a tree and hiked back to the cabin, where Sergeant Young was taking a siesta. He had given up the hunt because he hadn't seen any game.

Young and I started back to pick up the deer, and about

halfway we met McCartney with the carcass on his back. Mac was a wrestler and football player, with huge shoulders and a powerful frame, but in spite of his tremendous strength he was blowing and sweating under the load. When he saw relief on the way, he dropped the deer and collapsed on the trail.

After seeing a strong man like McCartney having trouble packing that deer I didn't feel so badly about returning for help. It was not the weight so much as it was the unwieldy bulk of the thing, for when Young and I lashed it to a pole which we carried between us, we easily made it back to camp.

A couple of years later, a sergeant from division headquarters named Crawford and I went back to the Mears ranch to try our luck. The pet buck had run off the spring before and hadn't come back, for the call of the wild was stronger than his appetite for the oats John Mears fed him. John wasn't able to go with us on this hunt, but I knew the country well enough to find our way so Crawford and I started out on our own.

The first day neither of us saw a deer, but there was plenty of sign and we knew there was a herd in the vicinity. The second morning we went out early to be in our stands at sunrise, but when noon came and we had not seen any game we started back to the cabin.

We had walked about half a mile along a ridge when a buck with a big rack of antlers broke out of the cedars on the slope below us and trotted across a clearing. He was only about a hundred yards from us, presenting a big target in the open. Releasing the safety on my Winchester, I picked out an imaginary bull's-eye on the buck's shoulder.

Try as I might, it was impossible for me to lift the rifle. Unable to move, I stood there as if hypnotized while the deer flicked his tail defiantly and disappeared in the brush.

As the white-tail vanished, Crawford came up behind me. "What's the matter?" he asked. "Why don't you shoot?"

Getting my wits under control, I remembered Joe Collins's explanation and muttered something unintelligible about buck fever. Sooner or later every hunter gets hit with it.

CHAPTER FOURTEEN

The Big Maneuver

In 1940, with World War II spreading over Europe, it began to look as though trouble was coming our way and soldiers of the regular army would have to start earning their wages. The jokes about backing up to the pay table to collect the few dollars we had coming each month stopped. They weren't funny anymore.

Since World War I the largest unit involved in field training, except on rare occasions, was the brigade, which went on maneuvers for a week or two annually. One exception was the motorized training of the 2d Division in 1938. With the reorganization of the infantry division in 1939 the two brigades were replaced by three infantry regiments and the entire division moved into the field.

In April, 1940, the 2d Infantry Division and the 1st Cavalry Division, which was stationed in Texas along the Mexican border, were ordered to Louisiana for joint maneuvers. This was the largest assemblage of U.S. troops since World War I; it included two of the four active divisions of the army. The others were the 1st in New York State and the 3d in Washington State.

In 1940 the cavalrymen still had their horses for it was not until 1942, when the mounted division went to the Pacific theater, that the oat-burners were discharged from the service and the troopers became foot soldiers to fight in the jungles of the Admiralty Islands and in the Philippines. In 1940 the .45-caliber Colt pistol was still being fired from the back of a galloping horse.

With the reorganization of the infantry division, the 3d Brigade was disbanded and Brigadier General Stilwell, the brigade commander, became the infantry commander of the 2d Division. Later this title was changed to assistant division commander. General Krueger continued as 2d Division commander.

General Stilwell was accompanied to division headquarters by his aide, Capt. Frank Dorn, his executive officer, Major Sandusky, and four enlisted men from 3d Brigade Headquarters Company. M. Sgt. Ed Ward, Privates first class Vincent Iarusso, John ("Jimmy") James, and I were the ones selected. Ed was on his seventh enlistment, Vincent his fifth, and I my third. Jimmy was on his first hitch.

The 2d Division made the move to Louisiana by motor convoy, traveling from Fort Sam to Bryan, Texas, the first day and camping in a field near the town. On the second day we reached the Angelina National Forest east of Lufkin and pitched pup tents near the Angelina River in a pine forest. These were leisurely motor marches, the spring weather was pleasant, and for infantry soldiers accustomed to long marches on foot it was a pleasure ride.

The 1st Cavalry Division traveled from the border stations, Forts Brown, MacIntosh, Ringgold, and Bliss, to the maneuver area in trucks, and the horses were hauled in vans. The horse artillery guns were towed by trucks, then hitched to the six-horse teams on arrival in the training area.

In 1940 western Louisiana was thinly populated, and only a few towns and settlements were located within the maneuver area. Most of the land was covered with pine, and one of our bivouac areas was in a virgin pine forest, the giant trees several feet in diameter with a thick bed of soft needles underneath which made a comfortable mattress. A few farms were scattered through the forest where the timber had been cleared and numerous sawmills were sawing lumber throughout the region.

There were snakes, too. There must have been more snakes per capita than any other place known to humankind for they thrived in the low, marshy swamps and in the many creeks and ditches. It wasn't that snakes were new to 2d Division men, it was that the Louisiana species were different. Texas was populated with huge, deadly diamondback rattlers and giant indigo snakes that looked fierce although they were harmless, but those Louisiana reptiles were sneaky as well as mean. The Louisiana coral snake didn't give a warning like a rattler and could slip up on a man, even get in his blankets without making a sound. They were deadly, too, worse than a rattler, and it was said that if bitten by one a man died a lingering death without hope of recovery. That was the story, and no one doubted it, but there were no deaths from snakebite in Louisiana just as there were none in Texas. Chiggers and poison ivy caused a lot more discomfort.

After a few days, when no one was bitten by a snake and the scare wore off, it was no longer a topic of conversation, but before a man bedded down for the night he took a careful look at the ground and shook his blankets to be on the safe side. There were a few brave souls who would hunt snakes for the skins to use as hatbands or to decorate riding crops, but there wasn't a lot of competition for the business.

The maneuver area lay between the towns of Mansfield and Leesville, a distance of some sixty miles. The training consisted of the two divisions advancing on such objectives as railroad stations, sawmills, crossroads, and settlements that lay in the line of march. The villages of Zwolle and Hornbeck were captured, occupied, and plundered numerous times by both divisions in the course of the exercise, theoretically, that is.

The nearest thing to actual looting occurred at a crossroads store in the woods when a column of 2d Division troops halted nearby. Some men went to the store to buy candy and soda pop, others followed, and the place was soon overrun with soldiers buying merchandise of all kinds. Tobacco and canned food were popular items. One man bought a kerosene lantern. Another bought a pair of knee-high rubber boots, perhaps with those snakes in mind. When the rest break was over and the troops moved on, the storekeeper was left with empty shelves but no doubt with an unexpected profit.

The combined force of the two divisions, infantry and cavalry, gave the appearance of an invasion force occupying the land. Horse cavalry rode along the gravel roads and through the forest, often moving at a trot across country. The six-horse teams pulling the cavalry division artillery lined the roads in long columns, sometimes unlimbering to allow the gunners to fire blank rounds to lend reality to the training. It was like a scene from a past war, before the motor vehicle replaced the horse.

One day I was standing by a road when a column of horse-drawn artillery marched by, gun crews riding the near (left) horses of each pair or perched on the caissons, when a farmer came out of a nearby field and looked enviously at the passing teams.

"Man," he said, "those horses are real pretty. I'd give anything to own a hitch like that. Do you think the army would sell some of them?"

I told them I didn't think they were for sale, and he said, "I've never seen horses like that before." He was a good judge of horseflesh.

For the enlisted soldier, living in the field on a two-division maneuver was no different than the usual field exercise of the regiment or brigade. Only the terrain was different. The tactical training was the same—the soldier's time was occupied with marching, setting up gun positions, maintaining communications with other units, moving supplies, and keeping healthy.

The division and maneuver headquarters staffs, on the other hand, were faced with the bigger problem of planning operations for what was now an army corps, an organization of two or more divisions. Use of the roads by an increased number of units required careful coordination, and more supplies were needed.

General Stilwell directed the tactical operations of the three infantry regiments and supervised field operations, assisted by his staff, Major Sandusky and Captain Dorn. Sergeant Ward was in charge at the command post. Vincent Iarusso, a topographical specialist, kept the situation map. Jimmy James kept the log of events. My duty was to keep communications open with the regiments and division staff sections by field telephone on lines provided by the division signal company. Setting up and moving General Stilwell's command post was also the duty of the enlisted men.

The general and his staff officers used a sedan for transportation. The enlisted section traveled in a vehicle called a command car. The command post equipment consisted of tents, field desks, and map boards hauled in a truck furnished by the division motor pool.

At the start of a training exercise we would set up the command post under the direction of Sergeant Ward, prepare the maps for use by the staff officers, and open communications. Pup tents would be pitched nearby. We took our meals with the division headquarters company, which might be located a quarter-mile away.

Vinegar Joe customarily would have his driver-orderly, Corporal Lanius, pitch his pup tent near the command post, along with the rest of the section. He seemed to like roughing it and spurned the larger tents and comfortable cots set up in the division staff area.

One morning after breakfast several officers who were visiting the command post got into a discussion of the Russo-Finnish War, which had ended shortly before.

"The Finns put up a great fight," one said in a sportsmanlike manner. "If they hadn't been outmanned and outgunned they might have beaten the Russians."

"Yes sir," another said, in sympathy with the underdog, "the Finns fought the Russians to a standstill as long as they could hold out. On equal terms it would have been a different story."

General Stilwell, busy at his morning exercise, stopped long enough to observe crisply, "The Finns got whipped. The idea is to win a war. Nothing else matters."

That stopped the conversation, but those words from Vinegar Joe stuck with me. In the Korean War, MacArthur put it another way: "There is no substitute for victory."

Around noon on Saturday, training would be called off until Monday morning and men of both divisions would head for the nearest town. Leesville was the favorite hangout, and soldiers would crowd into restaurants, stores, the movie house, or any place rumored to be of questionable repute, whether true or not.

Barbershops were popular, not only for haircuts but because they had bathrooms in the back of the shop where a man could clean up. Soap and towel were included for twenty-five cents. It was not a shortage of water in the maneuver area that prevented a man from taking a bath, it was those snakes.

Except for the merchants, the civilians avoided military personnel. In the 1920s and 1930s regular army soldiers were not given much respect by the public, and it took a war to change that feeling. We would joke about this attitude, attempting to make humorous comments and at the same time resenting it. "When soldiers come to town the womenfolk stay inside and lock the doors" was a favorite wisecrack. "Criminals, idiots, and soldiers are not allowed to vote here" was another. Or a man would say, "I heard a civilian swear that if he ever had a boy who stepped off with his left foot first he would drown him," referring to the practice of starting to march with the left foot. But the civilian world was different from ours—there didn't seem to be anyone in charge.

After wandering around town for several hours and spending what money we had, we would return to the outfit, sometimes walking for miles, but happy to have had a brief look at civilian life even though the women and girls kept off the streets.

At the end of April, when the big maneuver ended, the 1st Cavalry Division returned to the border posts, hauling the horses as before. The 2d Division was trucked to Fort Sam, where it was back to garrison routine once more, but the army was taking on a new look and the regulars began to get down to more serious business.

CHAPTER FIFTEEN

The New Army

In 1940, changes began to hit the troops in rapid succession, as if the high command knew trouble was coming but didn't want to let the people in the field know about it. Little by little, new equipment replaced old, new organizations were activated, and the pace of training picked up. One thing did not change—the pay remained the same, starting at twenty-one dollars per month plus bunk and three squares for a private.

One of the most radical changes was when the Garand M–1 replaced the Springfield rifle as the primary weapon of the infantry. Many old-timers didn't like the new rifle for it was poorly balanced, clumsy to handle, and couldn't pinpoint a shot like the Springfield, although it fired the same cartridge. Also, because it was semiautomatic firing, it ate ammunition faster than a recruit ate biscuits.

The Garand had one redeeming feature that made it acceptable—it didn't beat the shooter about the head and shoulders as unmercifully as the Springfield. For this reason it was popular with infantrymen who had been mauled by the older model.

But the new weapon committed mayhem on a soldier in another way because of the bolt operation. When the bolt was in the open position, the method of closing it was to hold the bolt handle with the side of the little finger of the right hand while releasing the magazine follower with the thumb of the same hand. This allowed the bolt to shoot forward into firing position, but the action was powered by a strong spring, and the bolt would mash a man's thumb unless he quickly jerked it out of the way. Until a soldier got the hang of this procedure, he would suffer from a bloody digit, referred to as "M-1 thumb," cursing the day the army made him trade in his reliable Springfield. Still, the Garand M-1 served honorably in World War II and in Korea, until it was replaced by even faster-firing rifles in Vietnam.

Another innovation was the new squad drill, designed to permit more rapid training of recruits. There was less criticism in the ranks about this change than about discarding the Springfield, for some of the improvements were obvious.

The new formation was less complicated and easier to learn than the old because the squad lined up in one rank of eight men instead of two ranks of four men each. On the other hand, it lacked military precision, as the men were strung out in an awkward line, but all agreed that that wasn't the most important thing about squad drill.

Even the proposal that a squad leader would have the rank of sergeant did not meet with the approval of all men in the ranks. Some thought a corporal had all the authority necessary to lead a squad and that another stripe would only go to his head. This reasoning was backed up by a bit of barrack philosophy that proved to be true in many cases: if a man who knew his job was promoted too fast, he got drunk with power; if a man who didn't know his job was promoted too fast, he just got drunk.

It was not until a rumor drifted down the chain of command that the squad would be increased from eight to ten men that the new drill was accepted without further argument. This removed all doubt as to which formation would be used. There was no way to form ten men in two ranks of four each.

So it came to pass that "squads east and west," as we derisively called the old drill, went the way of the wrap legging, the K-cart, the hand-powered radio telegraph, the Springfield rifle, the long bayonet, the washpan helmet, and other outmoded relics. The new drill was part of the new army, and we made the best of it.

A change that meant more to many men in the ranks, as well as officers, was the reorganization of the infantry division, which eliminated the brigades and reduced the four regiments to three, a move that required the transfer of personnel to make adjustments in job assignments. This affected the infantry organization only, for the artillery units remained much the same.

The 3d Brigade, my home for six years, was one of the first to case its colors, scattering the enlisted men of headquarters company to new billets. Some returned to their old regiments, the 9th and 23d; others wangled special duty jobs with corps area headquarters or went to the army air corps. A few transferred to Hawaii and the Philippines, little suspecting that in a couple of years they would have reason to doubt their judgment. I considered returning to the 9th Infantry because I still had friends there but instead went to 2d Division headquarters when offered a job in General Stilwell's office.

As regiments were shuffled in the reorganization, many men transferred for a variety of reasons that did not appear in the records. It was an opportunity for a man to make a fresh start with a new commanding officer or topkick, one who would not hold his past sins against him when a vacancy for a promotion came open. More than one unhappy shack man found it a good time to transfer to a distant outfit, leaving behind a woman who did not understand him or the army. Wandering soldiers with itchy feet used the reorganization as an opportunity to move on to new stations, look around, and, if they were not satisfied, move on again. There were plenty of jobs for a man with military training.

The change to three regiments in the division from four in two brigades worked out better than expected by the critics, who feared the elimination of the brigade formation would result in tactical confusion. In reality it proved to be much simpler because each of the three infantry regiments in the division contained three rifle battalions; each battalion was made up of three rifle platoons, and each platoon consisted of three squads. Hence the tactical rule of "two up, one back, hit 'em in the flank, then feed a hot meal' applied to all infantry units, made it simple to teach, and worked well in combat.

After the 3d Brigade was disbanded, the 2d Division did not seem the same to me, and when the 7th Division was activated in June, 1940, I requested a transfer to Camp Ord, California, where it was assembling. My request was approved, and I joined the 7th in July.

The regiments of the 7th were the 17th and the 32d, pulled in from small stations throughout the West, places like Fort Crook, Nebraska, and Fort Douglas, Utah, where those organizations had been scattered by companies and battalions since World War I. The third regiment was the 53d, made up of men who volunteered from other units.

The 7th Division was in good hands from the start—Vinegar Joe Stilwell was the commander. He was the same peppery leader who took a personal interest in the men under his command, and his enthusiasm carried down through the ranks. One day I met him on the road when he was inspecting the troops at training.

"How are things going, Sergeant?" he asked, returning my salute. "Everything all right?"

I reported that my section had good personnel, was comfortably quartered, and was glad to be in the new division. He nodded, spun around, and strode away to join a marching column of troops. It was only a brief greeting, but Vinegar Joe's cheerful words were a great morale builder and I told everyone in the outfit about it.

We were quartered in tents on the Ord Military Reservation, near the Presidio of Monterey, California. Now there was no time for horseplay; the training schedule was strenuous and the workday long. There were no afternoons off for athletics and only Saturday night in town to break the routine. No one thought of practical jokes or hazing recruits. The mood of the camp was one of sober attention to duty by all ranks.

Even the local saloons had a different atmosphere from the beer halls in San Antonio. There was less noise, and the customers wore coats and ties. Bill Rader, a buddy in division headquarters, and I ran into a soldier we knew in a Monterey hotel bar. "Gawdamighty," our friend said in surprise, "at first I thought you were a couple of bankers."

Comrades from other outfits joined the 7th Division from time to time. Red McCann, my platoon sergeant in Company A, 9th Infantry, transferred to the 17th Infantry Regiment.

"This is a different army," Red said, when I bumped into him one day. "Everything moves faster. In this outfit you don't obey an order until it is changed." It was good to see Red again.

The speed with which the army was expanding certainly indicated that the people at the top suspected something was going to break loose somewhere and were getting ready for it. The construction of new camps, the activation of units, the call-up of reserve and national guard personnel wasn't taking place without a good reason. Still, no information came down to the troops in the field that anything unusual was going on to explain all the hustle.

By the summer of 1940 military camps were springing up all around the country, with far more billets than men to fill them. The regular army had been authorized an increase to 175,000 enlisted men, and the ranks were still being filled by volunteers, with no talk of a draft. War did not seem likely, in spite of the trouble in Europe. I remembered that "tan plan" back in the company safe at Fort Sam Houston but shrugged it off and forgot it.

Construction of a large training center had begun in central California near the village of San Miguel, and there was talk of sending a cadre of officers and noncommissioned officers to open the camp within a few months. This information was not official; it came over the military grapevine. The new camp was to be named Camp Roberts.

The expansion of all U.S. military forces was now in full

swing, and it brought a change that became a personal matter to me. A letter came down from War Department announcing that regular army enlisted men could apply for assignment as commissioned officers. As this had always been one of my goals, I decided to put in my application.

When I told my best friends in the outfit, Bill Rader, Dave Lang, and Harry Halvorsen, all noncommissioned officers, what I planned to do, they thought it a great idea, but when I tried to convince them they should do the same, they only came up with excuses.

"My girl is in Frisco and I might be ordered to Texas."

"An officer has to buy his own uniforms and I don't have the money."

"Too much responsibility and work."

Then I tried to point out some of the advantages. "Look," I said, "all an officer does is hang around the club and draw his pay. There is nothing to it."

They agreed on that point. "That's right," one said, "if there was any work to it, they would have us doing it."

The logic of this argument was sound, but they wanted time to think about it. Later, all three received their commissions and had successful careers as officers.

Having made up my mind to apply for duty as an officer, I obtained a pass in October, 1940, to visit headquarters in San Francisco to see if my new assignment had been approved. There I was told that it would be only a few weeks until I would be discharged as staff sergeant and ordered to report to Camp Roberts as first lieutenant of infantry. Elated at the prospect of a new career in the army, I started back to the bus station for the return trip to Ord, and on the way, an incident occurred that explained many of the changes taking place in the military service.

On the sidewalk, stretching for several blocks, was a long line of young men, moving slowly into a large building. As I was in uniform, I drew a few curious glances, but that made no impression on me for in those days a soldier suit was somewhat unusual in the civilian world. Maybe these men were looking for jobs or signing up for college. It wasn't any of my business.

As I turned the corner a block beyond the end of the line, a young man bumped into me, looked me over, and asked, "Where am I supposed to sign up, soldier?"

"What?" I asked, puzzled. "Sign up? For what?"

"Quit your kidding," he said. "You know what I mean."

"I'm not kidding," I said truthfully. "I don't know what you're talking about."

"The draft," he said. "Where do I sign up for the draft?"

"Honest," I said. "I've never heard of it."

The young man looked at me with annoyance and disbelief. "Ha," he said. "You know what I mean, all right. Never mind, I'll find it." He dashed off as I wondered what all the fuss was about.

At the bus station I bought a newspaper, and the front page told the story. The Selective Service Act of 1940 had become law, and that day the first men were signing up for the draft. In the secluded world of the regular army I hadn't heard a word about it.

Epilogue

By the time of the Japanese attack at Pearl Harbor, the old army had been swallowed up by the Army of the United States, the official designation of the force made up of the regular army, the national guard, and the organized reserve corps. When the active divisions sent cadres of officers and enlisted men to training camps and new divisions, they were filled with draftees. Later the newly activated divisions were also required to send cadres to other units until the army reached its peak strength in 1945.

This repeated shifting of personnel from regular units into cadres soon spread thin the men with military service among the total number of divisions and supporting units. The 12,000 officers and 175,000 enlisted men of the old army were eventually absorbed into a force of more than 772,500 officers and 7,370,000 enlisted men.

A typical example is the 378th Infantry Regiment of the 95th Infantry Division, which was activated at Camp Swift, Texas, in April, 1942, and fought in the European theater of operations. Of the table of organization strength of 3,257 officers and enlisted men, which was seldom reached, fewer than two dozen, of which I was one, had regular army service. The remainder were from national guard units or the reserve corps or were draftees. This situation was normal for all divisions. It was truly an army of citizen soldiers.

Although weapons, transportation, and much of the equipment were new, the training of the infantry remained the same as before the war. As luck or army orders decreed, the 378th conducted field training at the Leon Springs Reservation and extended maneuvers in the Louisiana maneuver area before shipping out to the European theater. This was familiar terrain to me, and the 378th often marched over the same routes, dug foxholes in the identical spots, and set up guns in the same locations the 3d Brigade had used in peacetime.

Infantry tactics were the same. The assault was built around the principle of fire and movement of the rifle squad and platoon, supported by mortars and machine guns with field artillery in support. On defense we dug foxholes, constructed bunkers, and organized strongpoints and centers of resistance protected with barbed wire and land mines. There was nothing new in the training manuals.

But war is full of surprises, and the first combat order received by the 378th was to attack permanent fortifications consisting of stone and concrete gun emplacements connected by a communications system controlled from an underground central command post. Our orders were to attack and capture the city of Metz, France, an industrial center east of Paris on the Moselle River, which was reported to be impregnable because of its extensive defenses. The 378th had not received training for such an attack, but fortunately we had several weeks to prepare for the assault. Using the experience of other divisions that had encountered similar defenses, we jumped off on November 8, 1944, and after three weeks of fighting had driven the German defenders from the city.

The method that proved to be most effective against the defensive works was for a rifle squad to work close to the enemy gun position while covered by automatic weapons or bazooka fire, then place a satchel charge (a pack of TNT carried as a satchel) against the door of the fort, then detonate it. This would blow in the door, causing casualties by concussion. Another tactic was to throw a thermite grenade into a gun port or drop it down the ventilating pipe of an underground bunker, driving the defenders into the open.

Other methods were tried but were not as successful. The "snake," which consisted of bangalore torpedoes linked together, was designed to be pushed through barbed wire obstacles and mine fields, then detonated to clear a path to gun emplacements for riflemen. This proved ineffective and was abandoned because the snakes seldom worked as intended and the tank dozers used to push them often were not available when needed. The flamethrower was never used by the 378th against pill boxes or bunkers because reports from other units indicated it was unreliable.

An unusual situation arose during the fighting in Metz which required a different solution. There were large sewer mains underneath the city, and as the Germans withdrew to the east some of their troops were trapped below ground. We did not want to risk the lives of our men needlessly and sent a request to division supply for tear gas grenades to be dropped into the sewers to force the Germans to surrender. To our surprise, the division chemical officer refused to approve the use of tear gas because it would violate the rules of the Geneva Convention. So we bypassed the sewers, and the German troops surrendered when they became hungry.

The explanation for having tear gas in stock was interesting—it could be used against mutineers or civilian rioters but not against enemy soldiers.

Combat in large industrial areas encountered by the 378th presented problems requiring on-the-spot solutions because lessons in this type of warfare were not included in the training manuals. Basic infantry tactics using the rifle squad and platoon to infiltrate through railway yards, factories, and mines to drive the enemy into the open or force him to withdraw remained the best method. Old army training had stressed the importance of small-unit tactics and leadership, and in this type of combat, as well as in others, it proved to be the key to the success of the mission.

In open country such as we encountered east of Metz, where the enemy defended the high ground, standard infantry tactics were commonly used. The terrain between the Moselle and Saar rivers was not unlike the rolling country at the Leon Springs Reservation, with the exception that the trees were pines instead of oak and mesquite. It was a farming region, but the fields were deserted because winter was coming on, and few civilians were to be seen at any time in the combat zone. During the fighting the inhabitants would go into cellars for safety or pass through the lines to the rear and out of danger. In the coal mining country civilians would take refuge in mines and stay there until it was safe to come out.

Every eight or ten miles there would be a farm village of stone houses with narrow roads leading into the surrounding fields. As the Germans fell back to regroup east of the Saar, they would defend the villages until forced out or dig foxholes on the hilltops to delay us with automatic weapons fire, then withdraw again when we hit them in force.

In this region the common tactic was for the regiment to advance with two battalions abreast, keeping the third battalion in reserve. Each battalion would go into the attack with the same formation, two rifle companies abreast leading the assault on the German position, supported by mortars, machine guns, and artillery. The third rifle company would follow in battalion reserve. We had often practiced this movement in peacetime training, and it followed the rule of "two up, one back, hit 'em in the flank then feed a hot meal." It proved to be a sound principle and was effective.

Following War War II, the policy of dismantling the army after hostilities continued but to a lesser degree than in the past history of the United States. In 1946 the strength of the army dropped from over 8 million to under 2 million, and by 1950 it was under 600,000 officers and enlisted men.

This reduction was carried out although the army kept divisions on occupation duty in Europe, Japan, and Korea, and it was necessary to continue to draft men as replacements. With the beginning of the Korean War the buildup of our forces started all over again.

By 1949 not many men of the old army remained on duty. Some had not made it back from World War II; others had returned to civilian life. The 1st Cavalry Brigade, 1st Cavalry Division (dismounted), was on occupation duty in Japan with only a handful of officers and noncommissioned officers who had been in the military service before World War II.

The old army had completed its mission of training leaders and furnishing cadres for wartime divisions in the best tradition of the United States, and the time had come for the new army to take over that responsibility.

Appendix A

3D INFANTRY BRIGADE, 2D DIVISION
Fort Sam Houston, Texas

July, 1934 to October, 1939

HEADQUARTERS

Brigadier Generals, Brigade Commanders
Howland, Charles W.	1934
Ovenshine, A. T.	1935-37
Humphrey	1938-39
Stilwell, Joseph W.	1939, at time of deactivation of the brigade

Staff Officers
Clarkson, Percy W.	Major (later major general)
Craig	Captain
Dolph, Cyrus A. III	2nd Lieutenant (later major general), aide to General Ovenshine
Dorn, Frank	Captain (later brigadier general), aide to General Stilwell
Miller, Robert	Major (later colonel)
Tarpley	Captain

HEADQUARTERS COMPANY

Dunkleberg, W. E.	Captain (later brigadier general) 1934
Peploe, George B.	Captain (later lieutenant general) 1935-39

Master Sergeants
Howland, Oliver*	Brigade sergeant major
Ward, Edward*	Brigade sergeant major

First Sergeants
Travers, John	
Hollon, Harry*	
Collins, Joe	Technical sergeant, communications

---

*Later became a commissioned officer.

Sergeants

Carney, James*
Campbell
Loucks, Louis

Smith, Elmer
Waggoner, Clinton*

Corporals

Burns
Coulter
Howell, Harvey

Jones, William
Fuchs (veterinary service attached)

Privates first class, privates, and specialists

Allen*
Babcock
Belcher, John
Billingsley
Bradshaw
Brady
Bullock
Bush, Woodrow
Carpenter
Cooter*
Crawford, Mitchell
Damour
Dawson
Duprey
Edney
Fetty
Fraim
Gautier, Gervais
Gee, James
Gonzalez
Graham, James*
Greenacre
Grishem, James
Hamilton, Wash
Harber, Gene
Harrington
Houchens
Howery
Iarusso, Vincent
Inglet

Jeffrey-Smith, Charles
Jordan
Kline
Krauth
Kuykendall
Kulikofsky, John
Lange, John
Ledbetter
Lee, Boyce
Lisco
Linderman
Lisle
Maitland, William
Matlock, James*
McCool
McDaniel, Harmon
McDaniel, Raymond
McDaniel
McGaughey, Robert
Mitchell
Moerschbacher, Joe
Montgomery
Odell, George
Osborne
Pitts
Peterman
Ray, Ben
Reed
Ross

*Later became a commissioned officer.

Routt
Shaeffer, William
Smith, James
Smith, Hinch
Steed, John
Tinsley
Vogel, Victor*
Wakefield
Ward
Warren, Archie

Werner
Wheeler
Whitehead
Wilkins
Wilkinson
Williams
Wilson
Wilson
Wolcott
Zollers

---

*Later became a commissioned officer.

Appendix B

ORGANIZED August 11, 1917, in the regular army at Syracuse, New York, as the 1st Provisional Brigade
> *Redesignated* September 22, 1917, as Headquarters, 3d Infantry Brigade and assigned to the 2d Division
> *Redesignated* March 23, 1925, as Headquarters and Headquarters Company, 3d Brigade
> *Redesignated* August 24, 1936, as Headquarters and Headquarters Company, 3d Infantry Brigade

DISBANDED October 9, 1939, at Fort Sam Houston, Texas

RECONSTITUTED January 25, 1963, in the regular army; concurrently, redesignated as Headquarters and Headquarters Company, 3d Brigade, 2d Infantry Division and assigned to the 2d Infantry Division

ACTIVATED February 1, 1963, at Fort Benning, Georgia

Campaign Participation Credit
World War I
Aisne
Aisne-Marne
Lorraine 1918
Ile de France 1918
St. Mihiel
Meuse-Argonne

120

Index

Italicized page numbers refer to illustrations

Index

Soldiers of the Old Army was composed into type on a Linotronic digital phototypesetter in eleven point ITC Garamond with two points of spacing between the lines. ITC Garamond was also selected for display. The book was designed by Jim Billingsley, typeset by Insite Publishing Co., printed offset by Thomson-Shore, Inc., and bound by John H. Dekker & Sons, Inc. The paper on which this book is printed carries acid-free characteristics for an effective life of at least three hundred years.

Texas A&M University Press: College Station

124